TRAINING FOR CHANGE

TRAINING FOR CHANGE:

New approach to instruction and learning in working life

Yrjö Engeström

International Labour Office   Geneva

Engeström, Y.
Training for change: New approach to instruction and learning in working life
Geneva, International Labour Office, 1994

/Trainers manual/, /Learning/, /Teaching/, /Adult education/, /Training/, /Vocational training/.
06.08.1

ILO Cataloguing in Publication Data

Printed in Switzerland   VAU

MESSAGE

Training and instruction are playing a more and more important role in the ILO's technical cooperation programmes. It is not easy to convey the real message of the ILO's international labour standards at the practical level without proper and well-organized training workshops, seminars or courses. In implementing occupational safety and health projects and activities, training often takes a leading role. A good example of this is the ILO's WISE methodology which uses training as the main tool in improving occupational safety, health and working conditions in medium and small-scale industries.

This book, *Training for change*, is a welcome reference tool on the different training approaches which our department is using. I would like to thank the author and all the other persons who have contributed to finalizing this publication. I am sure that it will benefit not only occupational safety and health personnel in general, but a much wider audience working in the different fields of adult education.

Claude Dumont,
Director, Working Conditions
and Environment Department

The year 1993 was a year of change in many ways. The title of this book, *Training for change: New approach to instruction and learning in working life*, was not taken by chance. Adult education faces the challenge of renewal, not only in developing countries but also in industrialized countries. The instructional patterns exercised so widely in school teaching and applied in adult education are the main reasons for existing crises. "Learning for life" has remained as an empty phrase in school learning, where learning is aimed mainly at tests.

The International Labour Office (lLO) uses training as one of its main tools in transferring new knowledge and skills to developing countries. Over the years, different technical cooperation projects have organized several thousands of training courses, workshops and seminars. During the last ten years I have worked and lived in many developing countries. I am confident that the use of more effective training methods could have yielded even better results than the use of conventional approaches. This belief was the main reason why I contacted Professor Yrjö Engeström, an internationally recognized expert in adult education, and asked his advice in improving the training approach of the African Safety and Health Project (Training and Information), INT/89/M16/FIN. We came to the conclusion that it would be useful to have some pilot courses based on the latest developments in training and education.

The first pilot course was a great success. At the same time it revealed many obstacles to understanding the fundamental concepts of a cognitive view of learning presented during the course. After the first regional pilot course, a similar course was conducted in a modified form on the national level in Kenya and later in Ethiopia. These courses further strengthened the understanding that it is possible to make a change in participants' attitudes and work practices by using this new approach in training.

Training for change is an entirely new book which is largely based on research that has been published during the past ten years, and on experiences gained from the pilot "Training of trainers" courses in Africa during 1992-93.

Although our Project has used this training approach for training of factory inspectors and the representatives of employers' and workers' organizations, I am convinced of the effectiveness of this new training approach for all training areas in adult education, especially for vocational training. I recommend the use of this book broadly for trainers across substance areas, organizations and cultures.

The African Safety and Health Project acknowledges with gratitude the financial support provided by the Finnish International Development Agency (FINNIDA). I wish to express my appreciation to Professor Engeström for his effort, patience and understanding in taking into consideration the new aspects and modifications in finalizing this book. I also thank Mrs. Jane Haapiseva-Hunter for her distinguished work in translating the Finnish background texts into English. Last but not least, I wish to express very special thanks to course participants of the first "training of trainers" pilot course who gave a great practical input in proving this new approach to solid and functional training.

Geneva, January 1994   Antero Vähäpassi,
                                                        Chief Technical Adviser

CONTENTS

INTRODUCTION

Training for change is a guidebook for those in various organizations who plan education and teach adults or young people. It is written particularly with the needs of human resource development and personnel training in mind. Examples and illustrations have been selected accordingly.

The starting point is that teaching is a serious affair. One aims at real results in learning, not just at rotation from one class to the next or a quick run through lecture notes. The quality of instruction cannot be raised by odd tricks or by technical means alone. What is needed is theoretical insight into learning and teaching. Only such an outlook can help educational planners, instructors and trainers develop consistent and workable solutions in changing situations.

This book is not a collection of rules and recipes. It is rather a fairly rigorous presentation of a theory of learning and teaching. A systematic sequence of concepts is offered in order to aid analysis and planning of instruction. At the same time, practical examples are given as well as suggestions for useful applications.

The concepts and assumptions of the book are based on a cognitive view of learning and on the psychological theory of activity.[1] According to these, learning is meaningful construction and creative use of intelligent cognitive tools, both internal mental models and external instruments.[2] Learning is also participation, collaboration and dialogue in communities of practice.[3] Finally, learning is also criticism of the given, as well as innovation and creation of new ideas, artifacts and forms of practice.[4]

Learning, then, is not just the stocking up of ready-made facts for memory. Nor is it merely the exterior performance (reaction) elicited by reward and punishment (stimulus) conditioning. Nor can learning be reduced to emotional experience, spontaneous interaction, or unguided self-realization.

In this book prime attention is given to the contents and quality of learning and teaching. It is not important how many correct answers a student gives, but what one understands and how one thinks and works. It is short-sighted to evaluate teaching and learning on the basis of individual test scores only. In this book, teaching and learning are seen as vital forces in the renewal and transformation of collective practices, organizations, and cultures.

Training and instruction are dependent on the cultural and institutional contexts in which they are practised. The first chapter of this book discusses the characteristics of work-related training of adults and gives an overview of the book's conception of instruction.

Training and instruction aim at learning. Without understanding learning, there can be no solid basis for successful instruction. The second chapter focuses on preconditions and components of productive learning. Primary emphasis is given to investigative deep-level learning.

Investigative learning can take place without instruction, and instruction often takes place without investigative learning. However, instruction can also be an important source and driving force of productive deep-level learning. Chapter 3 analyses the principles of the type of instruction which elicits and supports investigative learning.

Instruction is directed toward objectives. But what are the functions of instructional objectives and how should good objectives be formulated? Chapter 4 discusses and answers these questions.

The quality of instruction is crucially dependent on its contents. How should instructional contents be selected and organized? This is the topic of Chapter 5.

Instruction uses various methods. How are they classified and what are the criteria for choosing appropriate methods? These themes are discussed in Chapter 6.

Objectives, contents and methods should follow the same logic. To achieve this, certain procedures and tools for planning instruction are needed. These are presented in Chapter 7.

No matter how good a plan one has, the practical implementation of instruction always requires skill and tact from the teacher. Instructional skills are discussed in Chapter 8.

Finally, in Chapter 9, the message of the book is condensed into a set of "golden rules of teaching". These rules are heuristic principles aimed at provoking thought and discussion, not recipes or articles of faith.

The ideas and instruments presented in this book have a lengthy history. In the late 1970s, I initiated together with a group of colleagues a new approach to work-related adult education in Finland. Key ideas of this approach were published in my book *Fundamentals of Instruction* in 1982.[5] The approach has been adopted and tested in dozens of organizations providing work-related training to adults, from trade unions to governmental departments and private companies.

Ten years passed after the publication of that Finnish book. During that time, the approach was significantly enriched and partially revised due to accumulated practical experiences and new developments in research in learning and instruction. In 1992, the writing of this book was prompted by a request from Antero Vähäpassi, director of the ILO's *African Safety and Health Project*. The project aims at helping factory inspectors in various African countries to redesign their work practices and to become effective instructors.

I conducted an intensive "training of trainers" pilot course for African factory inspectors in Harare, Zimbabwe. The first draft of this book was used as a course reading. The ideas of the book were put to practical test when the participants designed and implemented training courses in their respective countries and returned to report and evaluate them in the second part of the course. I thank Antero Vähäpassi and the participants of the course for their valuable feedback and ideas.

---

[1] For a general overview of the cognitive approach, see Gardner (1985). For an early formulation of the direction of cognitive theory adopted in this book, see Norman (1980). For general presentations of activity theory, see Leont'ev (1978); Vygotsky (1978); and Wertsch (1981).

[2] On the importance of tools and artifacts in human cognition, see Donald (1990) and Norman (1988).

[3] For analyses of learning as participation in communities of practice, see Schön (1983 and 1987) and Lave & Wenger (1991). For the collaborative nature of cognition, see Galegher, Kraut & Egido (1990) and Resnick, Levine & Teasley (1991). For the dialogical or multi-voiced nature of cognition, see Markova & Foppa (1990) and Wertsch (1991).

[4] On learning as creation, see Engeström (1987). On the differences and similarities of these three complementary forms of meaningful learning, see Engeström (1991b).

[5] Several editions of the book were published in Finnish; see Engeström (1982). Many central ideas and related research findings have been published in English in subsequent articles and books; see e.g., Engeström, Hakkarainen & Hedegaard (1984); Engeström & Hedegaard (1985); Engeström (1987); Engeström (1990). Recently Reijo Miettinen published a pioneering dissertation which reports and evaluates in detail the process and results of implementing the approach of this book in the instructional practice of a large training institute for teachers of commercial colleges in Finland (Miettinen, 1993).

EDUCATION, INSTRUCTION AND WORK-RELATED TRAINING

1

What is meant by education and instruction?

A person develops during his or her whole life span. Growth and development do not stop when a person reaches adulthood or begins a professional career. In many regards, the most important stage only begins at that point.

The development of the person as a member of the society is called *socialization*. It involves both unplanned or spontaneous and conscious and goal-oriented development. Conscious, goal-oriented influence on human development is called *education*. Along with education by parents and educational institutions, it includes a person's self-education, his or her personal efforts to attain development.

The education aimed at particular skills and competencies is called *training*. This is education which is aimed at the production of labour force for the various branches of economy.

There are two kinds of education. One is the influence people experience in the context of other activities. This happens, for instance, through games and hobbies, the arts and entertainment, or in connection with political activities. Most important is the education given in the context of work. Through job rotation, for example, the worker may get a chance to acquire new experience. Guidance and job-orientation, as well as performance evaluation, appreciation and criticism also fall within this kind of education.

When education is subordinated in this way to some other activity, it is mainly a tacit experience which regulates a person's development and forms the content of his or her learning. Learning is often incidental and piecemeal: it may happen practically without conscious efforts.

Another form of education is systematic *instruction*. Instruction, or teaching, aims at conscious, goal-directed learning. Its task is to motivate, direct and facilitate studying.

Instruction quite clearly differs from other forms of education mentioned above. It attempts to effectively influence the student's personality.

That is why it is typically separated from other activities and protected from disturbing factors.

In the case of instruction, what influences a person's development and forms the content of learning is *culture*, that is to say the accumulated and organized knowledge and skills embedded in the practices and artifacts of humankind and of the societies humans have fashioned. The main contents of instruction are not a person's own immediate experiences, but the experiences of others, stored in various forms of representation such as stories, books, pictures, models, instruments and computer programs.

This book concentrates on *teaching*. Activities aimed at human resource development involve many other means besides teaching. However, such other means are often most effective when connected to the systematic teaching of the intellectual foundations of work.

Characteristics of work-related training of adults

The training of working adults places its own particular demands on teaching. These may be characterized as follows:

o   A large part of instruction is commonly planned and executed by professionals whose main job is not instruction. Often an expert or functionary is only involved occasionally to lecture or carry out a limited sequence of training. Only a very small number of those involved in such training and teaching tasks have themselves studied educational or behavioural sciences.

o   On the other hand, people giving occasional instruction in their own fields are generally experts in the subject they are teaching. Lots of experience, conceptual mastery and informed opinions pertaining to contents of instruction are thus often readily available.

o   Teaching is generally linked to fairly evident functional needs and problems of an organization, so practical results and applications are demanded. This often affects how the theoretical bases of what is being taught are treated and developed.

o   The association with work practice gives a strong motivational base to studies. It provides a source of possible examples and tasks.

o   Contents, students and staff change continuously and are often mismatched. Training sessions usually last a short time and often remain isolated. So many different themes are treated that study may be rendered incoherent. In the time of a short course the material may not be internalized well enough so that one would gain independent command of it. This hampers its application in work practice.

o   Yet the short duration of training may increase intensity and prevent teaching from becoming tedious.

o   Professional training functions usually involve many planners and executors. The planner, the course leader and the lecturers may be all different individuals. This causes problems for the division of labour and for teamwork. The individual lecturer is not always able to connect his or her part of the subject matter to the overall theme, and the course leader may have inadequate knowledge of the content of the subjects treated.

o   On the other hand, the joint planning and realization of a training course make use of more diversified expertise than is possible in traditional school teaching under the wing of the single teacher.

o   Topics are often treated for which there does not yet exist knowledge based on solid research, or on which there are different, conflicting opinions. In teaching, this makes the presentation and consistent application of essential principles difficult.

o   On the other hand, the planning and realization of work-related adult training courses are often good occasions to develop, debate and test new ideas and explanatory models.

The particular characteristics of work-related adult training thus give rise to some problems, but they also provide new possibilities of developing high-quality teaching. These possibilities can be exploited and the problems overcome by increasing instructors' awareness of the inherent dynamics of and conditions for successful teaching. In other words, the quality of teaching work cannot be raised very much on the basis of each individual's own experiences. A common language is needed through which to systematically plan, evaluate, record, exchange and generalize experiences.

The development of a shared language for planning and evaluation presupposes knowledge of the *theory of instruction*. It is therefore not enough to gather different directives for use in varying teaching situations. Instructors should have the ability to derive and mould their own functional solutions from general principles of teaching. A person cannot possibly develop and keep in his or her mind fixed specific solutions for every possible teaching dilemma. The problems are innumerable and they cannot all be foreseen. Therefore there is a need to train and educate theoretically thinking instructors.

This guidebook's view of teaching

When a certain course was finished and the results were evaluated, the following observations were made:

For his presentation, lecturer N. N. got clearly the best evaluations from the course participants (there were six different lecturers).

A few weeks later, when the participants' ability to understand and apply what they had learned was checked, it appeared that the very things taught by lecturer N. N. were learned more poorly than any other sections of the course.

How can such incongruity occur?

When this question is put to those engaged in training, they generally answer in the following ways:

o   Obviously, N. N. was a funny guy, a good presenter and teller of jokes, but his charm and manner of presentation were in fact a cover-up.

o   N. N. obviously did not fully know his subject, nor could he give a clear overall picture of it, but made up for the lack by other showy means.

o   Perhaps N. N. stressed interesting and entertaining details, but did not bring out the essential matter.

o   N. N. maybe replaced actual teaching with pleasant group work and discussion in which finally nothing new was brought up.

o   Possibly N. N. did present in a convincing way, but resorted to the vocabulary of his particular field so that the participants held him as a great specialist, but could not really understand what he was saying.

Any one of these responses could be correct. They all point to the same direction, to the importance of mastering contents in teaching. Poor knowledge of the contents cannot be compensated by external tricks. The responses listed above also indicate the central importance of guiding the learning process of the students. Entertaining tricks can help one get along with one's listeners, but do not assure good learning.

Thus we come to the essential difference between the external and internal factors of teaching.

By external factors, we mean directly visible circumstances during the time of teaching, such as the observable behaviour of students, or observable forms of teaching (lecture, group work, etc.). When attention is focused exclusively on external factors, the immediate reactions of students, such as their approval and laughter, become more important than making sense of the contents of instruction. Such teaching is a package of techniques for managing the short-term surface behaviour of students.

This kind of an approach is a consequence of the fact that those who plan and carry out teaching lack a vision of learning as an active *process of constructive sense-making* in which the students endeavour to understand the subject matter.

The understanding and exploitation of internal factors of teaching, on the contrary, are based on the idea that learning is constructive and conscious long-term mental work. What happens in the students' minds is more important than how students react externally. The task of teaching is to set going, feed and direct the active mental work of the students.

This insight leads to a new view of the components of teaching. In the setting of objectives, it is not enough to describe students' external performance; it must be made clear on what explanatory models and modes of discourse the performance is to be based. In motivating students, the use of external stimuli, rewards and punishments, is not enough; one must find the intellectual conflicts and dilemmas by which to arouse the true interest of the students in the subject. Instructional subject matter must not be perceived as just dead material from a textbook; it is to be interpreted as principles, structures, and debates between viewpoints to be discovered beneath seemingly frozen texts. Teaching methods cannot be thought of merely as alternating forms and technical arrangements (lecture, group work, independent student assignments, etc.); the task and purpose of each teaching phase must be made clear as a step within a complex cycle of learning.

To improve the quality of teaching, it is decidedly important to differentiate between the external and internal factors of instruction. Productive planning and execution of teaching depends on the mastery of internal factors.

Nor can external factors, however, go unnoticed in productive teaching. Although they are secondary compared to the internal factors, they are still a necessary condition for good teaching. The teacher's good presentation skills or the efficient use of audiovisual equipment are examples of this. Alone they do not lead to productive learning, but if the internal factors of teaching are under control, then good presentation skills and visual aids are truly helpful. Presentation must only be carefully set in proportion to the requirements of subject matter content and constructive mental work of students, so that they do not break away as ends in themselves. Poor external factors, such as a teacher's unclear speech, can sometimes seriously hinder learning, even though the internal factors have been well thought through.

Diagram 1 depicts the system of external and internal factors. It also gives a general picture of the viewpoint presented in this book. There are concepts in the diagram, the exact contents of which will be explained later. The reader may already at this point check the meanings of the terms in the "Glossary" section at the back of the book. It contains a useful vocabulary for the entire reading of the book.

The diagram advances systematically in accordance with the planning phases of teaching, from the definition of objectives to the instructor's actions while teaching.

To achieve solid and applicable learning, one should shift the centre of gravity from external to internal factors. But when planning teaching based on internal factors, attention must also be paid to the proper exploitation of external factors. The elements of the diagram will be treated separately later on. But before that we must explain what we mean by *productive learning*. After all, instruction is given in order to achieve learning.

Diagram 1: The external and internal factors in teaching (1)

External factors (means by which students' observable behaviour and situation are controlled)	Internal factors (means by which students' mental work is guided)
Instructional objectives	
desired observable performances described in the form of behavioural objectives	contents to be mastered, described in the form of cognitive objectives, or orientation bases of performances
Study motivation	
stimuli, rewards and punishments to keep the attention of the students	students' interest in the subject matter awakened through intellectual confrontation and cognitive conflict
Choice of teaching content	
ready-made facts and performance schemes	models, principles, systems of ideas, and modes of discourse
Methods of teaching	
variable forms of teaching; entertainment; maintenance of momentary alertness; assurance of students' external activeness	stepwise realization of an entire cycle of learning by means of complete instructional treatment
Output of planning	
time schedule, lecture outline, transparencies	curriculum for a thematic unit of instruction, explaining the progress of teaching from the viewpoint of learning
The instructor in the teaching situation (teaching skills)	
presentation skills; command of immediate social interaction; organizational skills; audiovisual techniques	command of the content of the subject matter; flexible reliance on the curriculum; instructor's ethics

WHAT IS GOOD LEARNING ?

2

Limited notions of learning

Here are some common ideas about learning:[1]

Learning is the receiving and memorizing of factual knowledge.

Learning is practising skills by repeating the same tasks over and over, motivated by rewards which reinforce correct performance.

Learning is the appropriation of new attitudes and behavioural models based on emotional and social experience.

These traditional opinions about learning comprise several built-in assumptions and limitations:

o   The learning of knowledge and the learning of skills are separated from each other. Knowledge is treated as a collection of immovable, ready-made facts unconnected to activity; and skills are merely motor performances in which knowledge and thought have no part.

o   Likewise attitudes are held separate from knowledge, as questions of "pure" valuation.

o   Human memory is thought of as a kind of stock room, where knowledge is put. Thus it is supposed that the greater amount of individual facts a person remembers, the better he or she has learned.

o   The student is thought of as an object of external influence. His or her own consciousness, will, aims and activity are disregarded. The student is also seen as an individual separated from his or her social ties and communities of practice.

o   Learning is fragmented into separate recalled facts, performances, or experiences. Meaningful, comprehensive structures of knowledge, as well as broadly adaptive patterns of thought, discourse and activity are left aside.

The usual way of dividing learning into three "sectors" (knowledge, skills, attitudes) strengthens these misconceptions.

Learning is construction

In reality, learning is mental and practical activity of the student which is much more complicated than mere "reception" and "storing". The student literally *constructs* a picture of the world and forms explanatory models of its different phenomena. He or she always selects and interprets information, not working like a camera or tape recorder. The student always ends up correlating and merging newly acquired material into his or her ongoing activity and earlier constructions. The learner's activity and existing models orientate and direct his or her attention, selection and interpretation. New material again molds and transforms earlier structures and activity. Through this kind of interpretation and construction, *meaningful learning* occurs. Meaningfulness originates when new knowledge, new tasks, run into and merge with the learner's activity and former knowledge. The weaker these connections, the less meaningful the matter is to the student and the easier it is forgotten.

These facets of productive learning can most easily be observed in everyday situations where a person wants to find out the explanation to a problematic or intriguing phenomenon. The learner is a curious observer and problem-solver. The object of learning is a problem or a phenomenon asking for explanation. The learner does not approach the object empty-handed. He or she turns to tools, books, other people's explanations and other such sources of knowledge to explain and resolve the problem. Those sources of knowledge serve as instruments in learning. Learning takes place as cyclic movement between the learner, the object, and the instruments. This simple structure of an everyday learning situation is depicted in diagram 2.

Diagram 2: The structure of productive learning in everyday situations

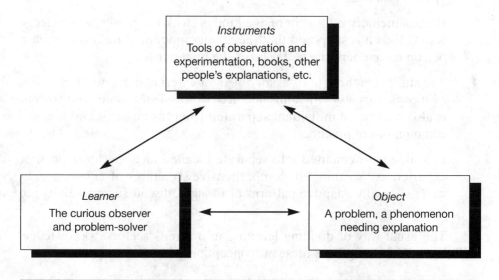

Although highly motivated and often innovative, everyday situations of productive learning tend to remain isolated incidents. They mostly result in relatively discrete and narrowly situation-bound insights. They are often interrupted or come to dead ends due to disturbances and lack of guidance. Instruction aiming at productive learning faces the task of overcoming these limitations of everyday learning without losing its strengths.

In productive learning, knowledge, skills and attitudes are closely merged together. Even while practising simple motor performances, a person is acquiring knowledge: an image or a tacit notion of how the motion is done is formed. Correspondingly, learning is always partial and contains a point of view, if not in any other way, in that it always expresses conscious or unconscious preferences of what things are important and what things are not. The explanation the student forms of a phenomenon is always an interpretation of it as well, and for that reason it contains at least a hidden emotional factor and evaluation.

Actions may be performed materially, with the help of external means, or on the mental, internal level. Ideas originate from the handling of material objects and phenomena. The source of mathematical concepts, for example, lies in the explanation of magnitudes and quantitative relationship of material objects with the help of material means.

The basis of learning is *internalization*, the transformation of material actions into mental actions. Language and speech play an important role in this process. Language is a tool by which material phenomena and acts are recognized and identified. With the help of language we gradually loosen ourselves from concrete, external means and switch over to performing actions with the help of abstract concepts.

A child learns first to count sticks or other material objects. Later he or she counts with fingers or with beads. Similarly, he or she counts aloud, using the help of speech. Gradually the child internalizes the process: counting begins to take place "in the head" and silently. However, pencil and paper, or a calculator, are still needed as a help in many counting and computing actions.

For adults, material objects can often be replaced by their representations, such as drawn or written models, performance instructions, etc. in the early stage of learning. Adult learning, however, also obeys the same internalization principle. When an adult learns to move in a new city, in the beginning he or she falls back on a material help: the map. Furthermore, he or she uses the help of speech: asks advice from passers-by, etc. Gradually he or she internalizes a model of the city. To choose a route has become an internal, mental action.

High quality knowledge

Knowledge is not comprised of fixed pieces. It exists in actions. Mastery of knowledge is manifested as actions, even though teaching often only recognizes the content of information, not the actions which require mastery. Weak and superficial knowledge is expressed in rudimentary actions: elementary associations and rote recall, naming of phenomena, description, comparison and classification. High quality knowledge manifests itself in the imagination and representation of complex processes and systems, in the analysis or separation of internal relationships and essential factors of a whole, in the formation and application of models, and in the production of new insights. High quality knowledge is organized in comprehensive constructs and models. It does not consist of isolated, separate details but integrates them into holistic and meaningful patterns.

Secondly, high quality knowledge is connected to living practice by multiple threads. It exists and develops as integral component and medium of practice. This does not mean that it has to be narrow and specific. In high quality knowledge, there is continuous two-way movement between concrete details and general principles. Thus, such knowledge can be broadly applied. It forms principles and concepts which can be modified and used in the solving of many different problems.

Thirdly, high quality knowledge takes multiple forms and is represented in multiple modalities. It is distributed between external artifacts, symbolic representations such as texts, mental models and images, and bodily actions and sensory experiences.

Fourthly, high quality knowledge is socially shared and develops through exchange, interaction and discourse between people. Communication and collaboration are crucial aspects of high quality knowledge.

Fifthly, by merit of the features enumerated above, high quality knowledge tends to have a long life and does not easily disappear from memory. Notice that here "memory" refers to both individual and collective means of storing and retrieving knowledge.[2]

These features give an image of high quality knowledge. But how is such knowledge acquired?

Types of learning

There is more than one type of learning. Depending on how narrow or wide the focus of learning is, different types or levels of learning may be distinguished.[3]

In *conditioning* by reward and punishment the student learns to react in a certain manner to a particular stimulus. This sort of learning has been abundantly studied in the observation of animals. It has been noted that by dividing the desired task into small parts and rewarding the animal's separate success in each partial performance, the animal can gradually be taught to repeat relatively complex multi-phase performances. Pigeons have been taught in this way to play ping-pong and dogs to dance – or rather to react to stimuli by performing these acts.

It is particular to conditioning that the learner does not need to be aware of his or her own learning. By his or her behaviour the learner aims first of all to escape disagreeable consequences and to secure pleasant experiences. This type of conditioning, adjustment to the immediate requirements of environment, occurs regularly in every person's normal daily life. For example, when a person notices that a certain way of greeting pleases his superior, he may begin to regularly greet him in this manner without specially thinking about it or recognizing that he has learned anything.

Processes of this type do not correspond to the characteristics of productive learning. What has been learnt is not organized into a whole structure, but endures as an isolated reflexive habit. It is not broadly applicable; on the contrary, a particular manner of greeting may please one person but irritate another. In practice such acquired behaviour may work, but it is strictly limited. When the foreman changes, new habits must be adopted.

Conditioning leaves unexploited the more important reserves which are peculiar to the human being: human consciousness, will, the ability to set objectives and to purposefully struggle to achieve them.

Imitation, in which the learner appropriates a certain behavioural model by imitating an example, is very similar to conditioning. It can be very effective and is largely the basis for influencing people through advertising and entertainment. Learning through imitation has been thoroughly studied in connection with the effect on viewers of violent television programmes. Studies have shown that though viewers may not consciously change their ideas, excessive watching of violent role models does shape their reactions and behaviour as such. Imitation, then, is learning which is only peripherally conscious or not at all so.

Both conditioning and imitation are forms of *first order learning*. The focus of learning is limited to the immediate performance or behavioural model at hand.

Diagram 3: The structure of traditional school learning

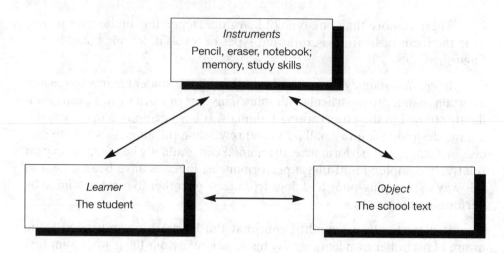

Traditional school instruction may be regarded as an example of first order learning. Students try to give correct answers to gain approval and avoid negative sanctions. They also imitate the performances of teachers and successful peers. The structure of such school learning differs significantly from that of everyday productive learning (see diagram 3).

In traditional school learning, the object is the school text, displayed in textbooks and in teachers' lecturing and dictating what are "correct answers". In other words, the authorized text replaces everyday problems and intriguing phenomena of the surrounding world as the object of learning. When the text becomes the object – an end in itself – it loses its instrumental character. This means that the students' instrumental resources are impoverished. Students are expected to rely mainly on their individual memories, and many tools are actually forbidden in traditional classrooms.[4]

While this type of first order learning goes on, a less obvious but much broader process of *second order learning* takes place in school, too. The students acquire general patterns of behaviour and thinking typical to the school context. They learn how to act and think like students, both overall and in specific subjects. This is sometimes called the "hidden curriculum".

In first order learning, the learner focuses on copying readily available correct behaviours. In second order learning, the focus is switched on to finding out how correct solutions can be produced even when they are not readily available for copying. Much of second order learning takes place through *trial and error*. The learner is vaguely aware of the task and the objective – for example of the implicit rules of acting and thinking like a successful student. However, the principles of such behaviour have not been discovered. Therefore the learner tries to find solutions by blind trials, sometimes succeeding, sometimes not.

TRAINING FOR CHANGE

Another form of second order learning is problem solving by experimentation or *investigative learning*. Here the learner pauses in order to reflect upon the problem and formulates a hypothetical explanation of the principles behind successful solutions. The learner then tests the hypothesis and modifies it according to the results. In other words, the learner constructs a theory of the phenomena under study. In school context, this would mean that the student analyses the preconditions of successful performance and consciously monitors his or her conduct and study habits accordingly.

Investigative learning clearly corresponds to the characteristics of productive learning. It requires breaking down and rearranging the structure of traditional school learning depicted in diagram 2. Its basic structure is similar to that of everyday productive learning situations depicted in diagram 1. However, it is significantly more complex because of its continuous nature which goes beyond isolated situations. Most of this book will focus on this productive type of second order learning and on the instructional solutions required to achieve it.

However, there are also processes of *third order learning* which will be briefly discussed at the end of this chapter. In third order learning, the learner questions the validity of tasks and problems posed by the context and begins to transform the context itself. In the school, this kind of *expansive learning* would mean that students and teachers analyse critically the practices of schooling and begin to transform their own practice. Obviously in such learning processes, internalization of given culture steps to the background while *externalization* of novel cultural practices gains priority.

Conditioning, imitation, trial and error, investigative learning, and expansive learning appear in many combinations. One type of learning may lead to another, and several types of learning run parallel in a community of practice. While all types of learning are necessary in human life, in instruction it is important to realize the qualitative leap that separates investigative and expansive learning from the other types. Researchers have characterized this leap as transition from surface-level to deep-level learning.

Surface-level and deep-level learning

Ference Marton and his colleagues have analysed students' assimilation and use of learning strategies.[5] The analyses throw light on the significance of the levels of learning.

The researchers observed that students, while reading a textbook, for example, follow two alternative strategies. The first is a surface-directed or *surface-level* learning strategy. The second is a depth-directed or *deep-level* learning strategy.

Illustrated with the example of studying a textbook, the characteristics of surface-level learning may be listed as follows:

o   the student tries to imprint the given text in his or her memory in the form it is presented in the textbook – he or she tries to function in the manner of a memory machine;

o   he or she advances in small incremental steps, focusing on one discrete piece of text at a time, often underlining the text paragraph by paragraph – his or her work is "atomistic", divided into small elements;

o   the student is not aware of his or her own method of studying and does not reflect upon the meaning and relevance of the contents of the text; the student pays more attention to how he or she will come through in a test or examination.

Characteristics of deep-level learning are strikingly different:

o   the student tries to go beneath the words, to understand what is meant by the text, what is its message and relevance;

o   he or she attempts from the beginning to create an overall picture of the content, to outline its structure, central concepts and principles, by carefully examining, for example, the introduction to the book and its table of contents, by leafing through it and by searching for key passages - his or her work is comprehensive or "holistic";

o   the student's manner of study is self-conscious and critical; above all, he or she tries to understand the content of the text and considers its veracity and usefulness.

Marton and his colleagues have established that as a result of surface-level learning, the student may have in his or her head, immediately after studying, a comparatively great number of separately recalled facts of what has been read. Deep-level learning, on the other hand, yields an essentially greater ability to analyse what has been studied, to organize it as a whole, to see its inner relations and to adapt it to new problems. Over time, such learning is also more economic in the recall of facts. Superficially learnt facts are quickly forgotten, whereas a profoundly assimilated construct connects facts to a meaningful whole and thus inhibits their being forgotten.

Surface-level learning is easily pumped in school, even in institutions of higher education. The problem is that once a strategy of surface-oriented learning has been adopted, it is very difficult to change to a depth-oriented strategy. Deep-level learning, on the contrary, is manifestly easily impaired or changed into superficial learning. Often all it needs is pressure for a test or examination, or the use of questions on a test which require only rote memory of separate facts.

Four conditions of investigative learning

Although not easy, it is possible to achieve consistent investigative deep-level learning. What is required for learning to be productive, investigative and depth-oriented? No single arrangement or method will suffice. The conditions of investigative learning must be designed as a system. There are four key components of such a system:

o first, the right kind of *learning motivation*;

o second, a proper *organization of contents* of subject matter;

o third, appropriate *advancing through the learning process*;

o fourth, adequate *social interaction* and *collaboration* in the learning process.

Each of these conditions will be discussed briefly in the next sections.

Learning motivation

Work-related adult training is mainly based on felt needs and problems in practice. Participation generally originates from interest in the subject being taught. In spite of this, motivational problems continue to exist even in training situations based on voluntary participation. Often trainers detect a peculiar phenomenon:

The people who applied for the course are stimulated by practical interest. From the first lecture on however, a familiar transformation takes place, as if the participants changed roles. They act no longer like active, working practitioners, but like traditional docile *students*. They seem to turn off to a minimum their mental ability to perform. The teacher tries everything to maintain and awaken the students' fading interest.

How can this phenomenon occur? The problem can be analysed by differentiating between the most important types of study motivation:

1. *Situational* motivation denotes the mainly temporary captivation of students' attention by external factors. For example, the fascinating novelty of a situation or subject, the external characteristics of teachers or other participants, the effective stimulation and entertaining performance used by teachers may all be a basis for such motivation. This kind of study motivation is of short duration, susceptible to disturbance and often directed to values only marginally relevant for the contents.

2. *Alienated or instrumental* motivation is based either on the goal of receiving external rewards or on the attempt to avoid failure and punish-

ment.[6] In school or college one often studies "for the sake of grades" or "to get through the exam". Interest is directed only to the reward in view or to the feared defeat, and their "exchange value". The exchange value of a certain result of an exam, for example, may be the open door to higher studies; or the exchange value of going through a certain course may be the chance to progress to a better paid job in professional life. When this is the dominant motive for studying, the student does not feel genuinely interested in the content and usefulness of the subject matter (although he or she may effectively pretend to be interested). Studying is uncritical, only aimed at getting done with and pulling through. Things are crammed into the student's head as easily and directly as possible, with no unnecessary reflection, and they are likely to be forgotten as soon as the test, exam, or course is over with.

3. Motivation is *substantial* when the study is founded on one's interest in the content and usefulness of the subject matter, when the student perceives its "use value" in mastering and understanding or developing and transforming the practices he or she is engaged in.

It appears that alienated or instrumental motivation is closely connected to surface-level learning. This does not mean, for instance, that the use of tests and grades leads automatically to alienated motivation and superficial learning. It leads easily to these if a strong, substantial motivation and a conscious interest in the contents has not been successfully awakened in the students. But if motivation is substantial, it does not necessarily suffer from tests and exams as such.

But how can substantial motivation be brought about? How to overcome the attitude of indifference and prevent the student from adopting already in school years the typical docile student role?

Different solutions to the problem of motivation have been proposed. According to one, the teacher should be a show-person who keeps students tuned in by giving them constantly changing stimuli and amusement. This model overlooks the possibility that students themselves could be interested in the content to be studied. As in entertainment, students remain objects. The entertainer's role is difficult: the public always wants new tricks.

Another proposal is to assure the motivation of students by taking their wishes as the basis for teaching. According to this view, it is dangerous for the teacher to set in motion his or her own instructional goals, for it leads to conflict with the wishes of the students and to their "intellectual opposition". "Fruitful and pleasant instruction" proposes rather that students be asked for their wishes either before or at the beginning of the training session. The teacher then selects those wishes which are not in conflict with his or her own goals, relinquishing however those goals which do not interest the students. Thus a harmonious situation and unanimity are achieved.

This way of thinking contains an faulty understanding of the significance of conflict for learning. Conflicts are seen as threatening and by all means to be avoided. The result is an accommodation to the subjective wishes of students, which often do not correspond to their genuine problems. Often people's most important work-related problems and needs are somewhat delicate issues, such as the feeling that one does not know how to master challenging and difficult tasks at work. For this reason students themselves when asked are not necessarily able to express outright what their needs are. They may not even be conscious of them, but reject them as too troublesome. A departure on the basis of subjective wishes, therefore, leads easily to a superficial, entertainment type of instruction and not at all to the appropriation of new powerful knowledge and skills, to the solving of demanding tasks.

To avoid conflict is in fact to underestimate students. When a student is facing a conflict between his or her way of functioning and in the demands of the new task, he or she does not automatically reject it. On the contrary, if such a conflict is appropriately calibrated and touches essential questions of the student's work, he or she takes it as a challenge. The student realizes that he or she must exert mental effort to solve the problem, to master new tasks and instruments.

Research points to the fact that conflicts, dilemmas and anomalies which are recognized as challenges are an important source of substantial, conscious motivation for learning.[7]

An example will show how these cognitive conflicts may be used in teaching:

According to several studies, roughly 90 per cent of car drivers are of the opinion that their driving skill is better than average. This is often not the case: they commonly overestimate their ability.

These drivers who overestimate their own skill are exactly those who would most badly need further driving instruction. Suppose they do come to a course: how can they be interested by what is taught? They already believe they are excellent drivers.

Will it help if the instructor assures them that the improvement of driving skill is very important? Hardly. What if the instructor presents a good show, tells them amusing anecdotes? The students might have fun, but they will hardly learn much. Will it help if they are asked what things they would like to learn? Hardly. They don't believe they have any need of learning exactly in the area where they have the greatest lacunae.

What then?

With the help of audio-visual equipment, for example, the student can be placed in simulated traffic and allowed to act in a precarious situation as best he or she thinks. Many students act incorrectly and are unable to avoid an accident. Once this is ascertained, together the instructor and student may begin to consider why. A conscious conflict arises, a crisis and a challenge. The instructor guides the discussion as to what principles a driver should observe to act correctly in a correspondingly dangerous situation. They then undertake to study just those principles and their application. A substantial interest in the subject has been aroused.

This is an example of a cognitive conflict based on a contradiction between what the student thinks he or she can do and his or her skill in an actual situation. There are several other types of potentially motivating contradictions. Dilemmas are one type; they are contradictory beliefs and accounts a person expresses of one and the same phenomenon.[8]

Contradictory explanations or competing ideas presented in study materials, argued and discovered by students in conversation, or suggested by the instructor are another type. Also practical tasks and objects of the outside world, such as social roles and institutions, are often inherently contradictory.

In order to become a source of substantial learning motivation, any one of these contradictions must be noticed, faced, and experienced by the learner as a personal challenge. Typically such an experience means that the learner is made to recognize a conflict between his or her existing skill or knowledge and the demands of the new concrete task.

Now we can further define the psychological conditions for creating a substantial study motivation.

1. A substantial motivation arises when the student experiences and recognizes a conflict between his or her knowledge or skill, and the requirements of the new task he or she is facing. The student stops before a problem and observes that he or she cannot pull through it any other way but by critically evaluating his or her own knowledge and skill. The curiosity is awakened and the student is prompted to ask: Why did I not succeed in the task? Why is it difficult for me? The need arises in the student to understand and solve the problem right to the roots. One can arrive thus far by using different tasks and problem situations. A conflict may be brought out on several different levels. It may stem from two seemingly correct explanations of a phenomenon which do not accord between each other and from practical experiments with these explanations. It may also stem from prejudices and preconceived attitudes of students which are in opposition to observed reality.

2. A conflict which gives rise to substantial motivation must be *central* to the students' work and needs and the contents of the subject matter. This demands a careful analysis of the contradictions and problems in students' work practice, of their former frames of knowledge, and of the new structure being taught.

The purpose of using conflict for motivation is to get students to consider core questions of their practice and of the subject matter. Thus in the example of driver instruction described above, the danger had to be such as is met with in reality. Furthermore, it had to direct attention to just those principles which were going to be taught, not to secondary matters. For this to take place, typical accident occurrences have to be analysed beforehand and information must be gathered about characteristic models linked to driving behaviour. Sometimes this kind of information can be gleaned from available studies; often, however, the teachers themselves must gather it.

3. Besides being attuned to a conflict which motivates them, students must be indicated what kind of principles and concepts they should construct in order to explain the conflict and eventually master similar problem situations independently. The formation of substantial motivation presupposes that while solving a problem, students form a general model of explanation, an *orientation basis*, valid for the content of what is to be learned. The identification of such a starting point arouses confidence in the possibility of gaining mastery over the challenging new territory of knowledge.

4. Students must also from the beginning get to use the models they construct in solving new problems and tasks. Only with this kind of *practical activity* will study motives be strengthened and long-term, independent interest for the subject be developed.

5. Students should eventually find that they master and can use the knowledge acquired, that they understand the matter and have some control over it. This organizes and crystallizes the contents learned and provides a strong basis for further study. Before long the students must face new conflicts which lead the learning forward.

To awaken substantial motivation in the students, the instructor must set high demands and challenges before them which require deliberate intellectual and practical effort. Instruction must go before learning, leading students into new, unknown territory. This implies an inevitable tension – the instructor knows at least some aspects and parts of the territory better than students. This tension is not to be evaded or hidden in the name of equality – it should be consciously exploited.

This view of learning motivation is pictured in diagram 4, which modifies the model presented in diagram 2.

Notice that diagram 4 speaks of mastering the conflict, not only solving it. This means that long-term substantial study motivation cannot be built only on isolated intriguing conflicts and clever solutions to them. To evoke deep-level investigative learning, a cognitive conflict must lead to the contradictions behind it. In the case of the drivers' training course, it is not enough that solutions are found to the initial problem situation that created the

Diagram 4: Cognitive conflict as a source of substantial learning motivation

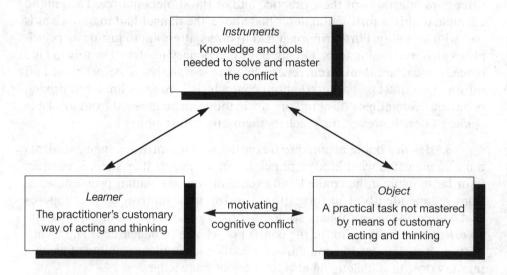

cognitive conflict. The much broader contradiction between the learners' overly optimistic beliefs and their actual driving performance must be uncovered, acknowledged and mastered.

Such an appropriate use of cognitive conflicts as sources of motivation creates a *context of criticism* at the beginning of the process of investigative learning. Students become aware of limits and contradictions in their practice and in the knowledge and tools they routinely use. Such a critical stance lays a vitally important groundwork for the construction of new knowledge and new forms of practice.

Representation and organization of knowledge

The content of learning is usually thought of as disparate facts stored away in memory like things in boxes on shelves. That this is an erroneous concept has been asserted above. In reality, people construct *models* of the world while learning. Models here refer to relatively stable patterns of thought and action.

Learnt matter and the corresponding models are *represented* in different ways. For instructional purposes, three main forms can be distinguished: a sensory-motor or physical representation, a visual or pictorial representation, and a linguistic, verbal representation.[9] Models can be expressed and acquired in direct practice, for example as performance routines in the work for which one is training. Models can also be expressed and acquired in illustrations, pictures and diagrams supported by imagination and mental images. Finally, knowledge can be expressed and acquired with the help of language and symbols in abstract and generalized form.

More fine-grained analyses reveal many intermediate or transitional forms of representation, such as gestures and metaphors. Within the main types, important further distinctions may be made, such as the distinction between narrative and categorizing modes of verbal representation. Finally, new media like computers and video discs offer possibilities of powerful hybrid forms of representation, such as multi-modal simulations and "virtual worlds". From the instructional viewpoint, it is important to realize and exploit the rich variety of representational forms and media without turning this variety into an end in itself.[10]

Our representations are often called mental models.[11] However, this is a somewhat misleading notion. The models by which we represent the world are in constant movement between the external and internal spheres: from externally visible bodily movements and postures to internal sensations and feelings and vice versa; from external pictures to mental images and vice versa; from verbal or mathematical thought to written text and vice versa. Thus, models are not exclusively individual and private; they are also shared cultural patterns of thought and action.[12]

Another dimension of the quality of models concerns the way in which they are *organized*. The simplest type of knowledge organization is that of singular facts, isolated characteristics associated with particular objects. A step up in the complexity of knowledge organization is taken by classifying objects on the basis of their general (necessary and sufficient) characteristics and by thus forming general categories and definitions. Ducks, chickens, cows and pigs are part of the overall concept "domestic animals". But ducks and chickens are birds, cows and pigs are mammals: by using another basis of classification, we get two other general categories.

Facts and classifications are insufficient when procedures and processes must be described. Procedural knowledge is typically represented as series of successive steps required to perform a task or to complete a process. Often this type of models are represented in the form of instructions, typically found in manuals attached to machines and technical devices.

A quite different way to organize knowledge is to fashion systemic entities or networks indicating the functional connections and interactions of influential factors in some complex phenomenon. From the point of view of learning, this kind of system configuration has often decisive advantages over classifications and procedural descriptions. Classifications are static, systems models are dynamic. Procedural descriptions are also dynamic, but they are

Diagram 5: How knowledge is represented and organized

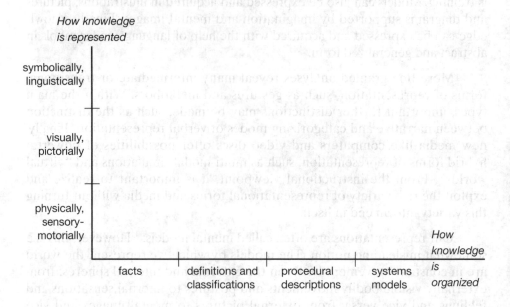

one-dimensional, restricted to one correct procedure. Systems models allow for seeking multiple alternative solutions. Thought wanders through the system and moves according to the functioning of the system, which contributes to further understanding, retention and applicability of knowledge.

The two dimensions of the quality of knowledge, how it is represented and how it is organized, are shown in diagram 5.

The teaching and learning of different intellectual models and constructs can be evaluated within the dimensions seen in the diagram. For instance, much of the information taught in school is described pictorially and linguistically, yet it is organized in single, separate, loosely organized pieces, as well as definitions and classifications which easily lead to rote memorization.

No type of knowledge representation and organization is universally better than others. Good learning requires flexibility and movement of knowledge in both dimensions. It is important that material actions be the basis of verbal information, for they disclose the origins of concepts. Correspondingly, streamlined, effective operations are needed for many work performances, but their elastic transformation in situations of disturbance requires that the principles behind the movements be understood and managed conceptually.

Jerome Bruner has appropriately characterized the significance of structured models for the assimilation of knowledge:

"Knowledge acquired without sufficient structure to tie it together is knowledge that is likely to be forgotten. An unconnected set of facts has a pitifully short half-life in memory. Organizing facts in terms of principles and ideas from which they may be inferred is the only known way of reducing the quick rate of loss of human memory."[13]

This assertion of Bruner indicates a close interconnection between the way knowledge is organized and the *explanatory depth* of that knowledge. The mere description of a phenomenon or task, the listing and classifying of its various external characteristics and distinctions represent superficial levels of explanatory depth. These levels do not answer the question, why the phenomenon or performance is what it is. The domain where knowledge can be applied is limited: the phenomenon or performance in question may be mastered, but the models acquired are of little help in trying to explain and solve new problems.

One may also explain one phenomenon by another which either presupposes or follows from it. This kind of consecutive representation is necessary for analysing and controlling the sequence of events in various processes. To assert consecutiveness is not yet to explain the reason for a phenomenon. Belief that it does easily leads to misconceptions, such as to think that "the sun shines so that flowers will grow".

Deeper explanation requires the explication of the *source, emergence and evolution* of a whole phenomenon or performance, that is of the system under examination. This way one can find general principles which influence phenomena and processes.

The search for such general principles and generative causes is particularly important for learning, for they have a large transfer potential. With their help, one can understand and master in principle an unlimited number of new individual problems and phenomena. In this sense they help produce new knowledge, enabling creative activity.

The following examples serve to illustrate the importance of explanatory depth.

Example 1

The purpose is to teach students how to use an internal-combustion engine. The task may be approached in different manners. Usually one proceeds by describing and showing the most often needed operations and the parts of the engine concerned. In this way the students learn to repeat the procedures set forth without really understanding why they are necessary.

Let us suppose that a student asks "Why does one start the motor in that particular way?" or "Why can't it be given a lower octane fuel?"

Of course, one could respond by describing the links between consecutive phenomena. For example: "Since the connection to the battery runs from there, from which electricity gets to the starter, which..." or: "Because it doesn't run or runs poorly on low octane fuel."

These only seem to be explanations. They cannot be generalized because they do not reveal the motor's functional principles. Only when the principles which govern the functioning of the motor are set forth can one understand the meaning and purpose of all the individual parts taken separately and with respect to the whole motor. Comprehension of principles also enables students to produce their own explanations and solutions to various unprecedented disturbances in the motor. Thereby they can quickly teach themselves how to handle problems in different motors.

The principle of a motor is comprehended when the origin of the internal-combustion engine is explained. What problem needed to be solved by inventing the internal-combustion engine? What was the solution? What basic insight was the point of departure for the engine's construction?

Example 2

The purpose of the course is to teach new factory inspectors to carry out safety and health inspections in various workplaces. A traditional way of teaching would focus on a sequence of steps deemed necessary in an inspection, starting with planning and gathering background information, and ending with writing and filing an inspection report.

While this kind of teaching might give the students a technique they could follow, they would not get an idea of why the inspection should be carried out just that way and whether there are alternative procedures to be pursued in some circumstances. The result could easily be a rigid adherence to a procedure without an insight into the "philosophy" of inspection work.

An alternative way of teaching the inspectors would be to trace the evolution of historical types of inspection work and their respective ideologies, goals and instruments. On the basis of such broader framework, various procedures for carrying out inspections could be acquired without becoming overly dependent on any particular procedure or technique.[14]

Explanatory depth of knowledge relates to different types of practical competence at work. Donald Schön distinguishes between technical rationality, based on fixed facts and solution recipes, and reflective rationality which requires flexible reframing of problem situations by means of seeing them holistically in their broader context. Shoshana Zuboff differentiates between traditional action-centred skills and new intellective skills demanded in particular by information technologies at work. The former are largely tacit, based on direct experience and difficult to communicate. The latter are based on collaborative analysis and exchange of symbolically mediated information, typically computerized text.[15]

Experience-based tacit skill is not enough in rapidly changing work conditions entailing many new, surprising problems. Not only technology but also legislation, to take an example, is so complicated and continually under change that the practitioner who attempts to get by at any given time by depending on his or her experience and memory alone is in deep trouble. It is simply not possible to depend upon a "ready recipe". Problems and novel situations are so numerous that there hardly are any immutable directives.

So far we have emphasized the importance of models and explanatory principles. There is another important, although much less known aspect to the organization of learning contents, namely the *modes of discourse* to be acquired. The realization of the importance of discourse in human cognition has been called "the second cognitive revolution".[16]

By modes of discourse we mean repertoires of talking, writing, and generally communicating meaningfully in a community of practice. Such discursive repertoires are not reducible to models and representations. Each community develops a "social language" of its own over time, with its typical vocabulary and attached typical meanings. Similarly, communities of practice also adopt typical "speech genres", routinized expressions and idioms which are repeatedly used as means of dealing with problematic situations. The talk and writing of physicians and lawyers are good examples of strong social languages and speech genres.[17]

Modes of discourse may be crucial mediating devices in the choice of practical actions. C. Wright Mills pointed this out as follows:

"Men discern situations with particular vocabularies, and it is in terms of some delimited vocabulary that they anticipate consequences of conduct. Stable vocabularies of motives link anticipated consequences and specific actions."[18]

Learning always entails acquisition of social languages and speech genres. For investigative learning, the modes of discourse of a given practice or field of study are vitally important toolkits. Instead of taking them for granted, learners should be aware of their potentials and limitations.

Modes of discourse are also modes of argumentation. Human communication always consists of meetings and clashes between points of view. Acquiring modes of discourse means learning to formulate and argue viewpoints. It implies that all knowledge, all learning contents are taken not as given truths but as historical and ongoing lines of argumentation between multiple viewpoints.[19]

Diagram 6: Dimensions of organizing learning contents

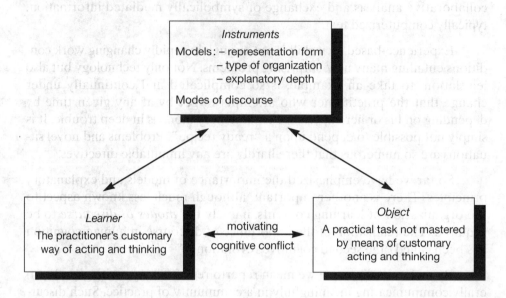

We can now summarize the significant dimensions of organizing learning contents with the help of diagram 6.

In investigative learning, contents are instruments of discovery, not ends in themselves. Contents are sought as means for solving and mastering cognitive conflicts that motivate learning. In this sense, the unfolding and appropriation of learning contents forms a *context of discovery* in the learning process.

Advancing through the learning cycle

Learning is commonly thought of as the reception of information through the different senses and storing it in memory.

Earlier we asserted that this portrayal of the learning process is inadequate. Investigative learning involves facing cognitive conflicts as well as selecting, organizing, interpreting, and appropriating new models and modes of discourse to master those conflicts. While learning, a person constructs his or her version of the subject matter, formulates his or her theory of the domain. In investigative learning, the learner also applies the new knowledge to novel problems, using it as a tool and resource. Learning becomes an ongoing process of questioning, discovering, and changing both oneself and the world.

But how can this ideal be practically accomplished? What steps are needed? We can approach these questions by studying the weaknesses typical of traditional training sessions.

Example 1

Lecturer A. A. holds a particularly interesting lecture on the possibilities of improving office work in government bureaus and institutions. Many questions are raised in the minds of the audience. At the end of the lecture the reserved 15 minutes have been used for discussion and questions. This is followed by group work with the theme "Charting the problems in our office". After reporting the groups' results, a new topic is taken up by a different lecturer.

The participants have the feeling that somehow the subject of "improvement in office work" has been left off in midstream. They are not really sure what they finally learned about it. One consoles himself by remarking: "Plenty of stimulating points were raised, even though I wouldn't know how to directly apply them…"

Example 2

Lecturer K. K. begins his presentation concerning water legislation by "going straight to the point". He sets out at the first paragraph of the law and goes systematically right through it.

The participants diligently take down notes and try to follow the rapid flow of explication. The lecture includes many new facts, isolated points and examples. After the lecture, the participants exclaim, "What an iron ration of important information!" Their perception of the subject matter as an ordered whole, however, is considerably vague, and in their thinking, the content of each section is mixed into porridge. Many participants have some difficulty in understanding what was important about the water law in question and why it was explained to them so thoroughly.

In the first example, learning was clearly left incomplete. The contents were not sufficiently digested, and what is worse, cannot be meaningfully used for solving concrete tasks. The participants tried to internalize the new information, but were not given a chance to methodically externalize it, or to try it out. The loosely specified group work did not really help: its content was not consistently linked to the testing or utilization of any principle learnt from the lecture.

In the second example, the situation was perhaps even more serious. In the first, the lecturer A. A. had obviously somehow managed to motivate the students; in the second, the lecturer on water laws went "straight to the point" and did not even try to interest the students in the subject or orientate them towards a general picture of it.

In the second example the learning process was directed to the surface from the beginning. Learning was lacking a meaningful framework. The students were not given any kind of "lens" through which they could have studied the new knowledge and organized it. Internalization was therefore a mechanical reproduction: it remained superficial.

Thus we come to the question of an *integral learning process*. In the examples given, learning was incomplete. What is meant by complete learning? It can be defined as learning which leads to high quality knowledge and above all, to the independent mastery of the subject matter and the ability to apply it flexibly in new situations.

The integral learning process is much more complex and requires more time than is usually acknowledged. The Russian psychologist and educator V. V. Davydov has formulated a theory of such long-term, complex learning activity. He divides learning activity into six learning actions. The following model of the integral learning cycle and its six steps is largely inspired by Davydov's work, although it differs from it in significant details.[20]

In an integral learning process, or learning activity, the student is an investigator looking for a broadly applicable and functioning explanatory model of some phenomena, trying out this model in practice, criticizing and correcting it. The process can be divided into *steps,* each demanding specific *learning actions*. The steps are the following:

1. *Motivation*: The awakening of conscious, substantial interest in the subject. It presupposes that the student experiences and recognizes a cognitive conflict. The conflict is recognized in a practical problem situation, in searching for solution, for which the student's former conceptions do not suffice.

2. *Orientation*: The formation of a preliminary hypothesis, an orientation basis, which explains the principle and structure of the knowledge necessary for solving the problem. It is important that the student analyses the problematic phenomenon as an active system and searches for the internal relations of the system, for its primary determinants. The student fashions for himself a "lens" for the assimilation of knowledge and the resolution of related tasks. It is an explanatory and active model which helps the student to see and select the essential points of concern and to link them together. This model is represented in material, external form, for instance as a diagram.

3. *Internalization*: The enrichment of the preliminary model with the help of new knowledge. The learner interprets and merges new information into the model, at the same time examining the properties of the model itself.

In practice, internalization occurs by using the explanatory model or orientation basis to organize and explain the parts and details of a system. The external model is gradually transformed into the student's internal model. Internalization may be brought to the point where certain performances are made automatic. These become shorter and quicker when they no longer require conscious reflection. They may, however, be externalized again in a problem situation and returned to the level of conscious thought.

4. *Externalization*: The application of the model as a tool in solving concrete problems with it, influencing change in the surrounding reality and producing innovation. Externalization is of decisive importance for testing and evaluating the model. It is also a necessary condition for the successful internalization of a model. Internalization and externalization are therefore inseparably linked to each other in an integral learning process. In practice externalization occurs when the learner, pondering a solution for a problem, reconstructs his or her explanatory model with the help of speech, diagrams, plans, sketches, and material actions. The theoretical principle of the subject must be transformed into practice so that theory begins to live and truly interact with action. Application enriches and corrects theory, raises new questions and compels creativity.

5. *Critique*: The student evaluates critically the validity and usefulness of the explanatory model he or she has acquired. The student checks the model's weaknesses and lacunae by using it in performing tasks and explaining manifestations of the system under study. He or she tries to determine its limits of applicability and to find possible problems for which the model would need to be extended or revised.

6. *Control*: The student examines his or her own learning. The student stops to analyse his or her ideas and performance in the light of the new model and corrects them according to need. The student checks his or her methods of organizing and interpreting information and solving tasks on the basis of the newly acquired knowledge. The student consciously tries to improve his or her learning methods. The student analyses the outcomes and products of his or her learning, identifying mistakes and strong points.[21]

The starting point of the integral learning process is therefore a true problem and a conflict raised in the student's consciousness. Following this, the student draws up a general model to clear up the conflict. This orientation step also occurs in practical activity, in a search for the explanation and answer to the question "why". A groundwork model of explanation is formed, a hypothesis, an orientation basis, which helps to organize and interpret the whole subject under study. It also helps the student to change his or her earlier understanding and way of dealing with the problem. During a period of comparison, examination and enrichment, the full meaning of the new subject matter takes shape – internalization occurs. At this stage, the decisively important testing and application of the new knowledge begins. The model must be used in performing concrete tasks, changing surrounding reality and creating new solutions – externalization. The possibility is opened for the student to evaluate critically the model and to control and correct his or her learning.

Learning in which some of these steps are weak or absent easily remains superficial and fragmented. Students may feel they have understood the subject, but when they are asked to externalize it, even on paper in free style, they realize that something was left off halfway. Knowledge is unsubstantial and tentative, its internal relationships unclear, and practical application is haphazard.

Models that describe reality are always abstractions and reductions. They generalize the components of a group of phenomena in an attempt to present the most essential of them. Learning is not limited, however, to interaction between the learner and the models which describe reality. A third essential factor is involved: reality itself, or practice. As already stated, the integral learning process sets out from practice, from an encounter with a practical problem which causes a conflict. Analysing this conflict in conceptual form and shaping a model to resolve it (orientation basis) shifts the focus of learning on to interaction between the student and the subject matter.

An integral learning process also leads back to reality and practice, at a new level. Models are tested and applied in solving novel tasks; in this way one tries to bring theory and practice together, to fertilize both.

All of the foregoing leads us to depict integral learning as a cycle or spiral consisting of the six steps described above. In diagram 7, the arrows indicate the student's learning actions in the successive steps. Step 1 at the beginning of the inner ring represents the student's substantial motivation evoked through a cognitive conflict. The student shapes a model for a solution of the conflict, forms an orientation basis (step 2). He or she enriches and internalizes it (step 3). Internalization, in fact, is closely related to externalization and task performance, presented by the first phase of the outer ring (step 4). The solution of tasks by using the knowledge acquired leads to the critical evaluation of that knowledge and its eventual revision (step 5), and to the learner's control of his or her own learning and its results.

The cyclic or spiral illustration is somewhat simplistic and mechanical. In fact, movement along its rings runs constantly both directions and the different phases are often parallel. But simplified as it is, the illustration serves to show what an exacting affair the investigative learning process can be. It offers no short cuts.

In diagram 7, the dotted lines indicate components that are embedded in and interact with larger entities. Thus, the initial motivating task or problem is embedded in the broader practice to be mastered; the orientation basis is embedded in the broader set of tools and knowledge to be acquired; and the new ways of acting and thinking the learner internalizes are embedded in his or her customary ways.

Diagram 7: The cycle of investigative learning [22]

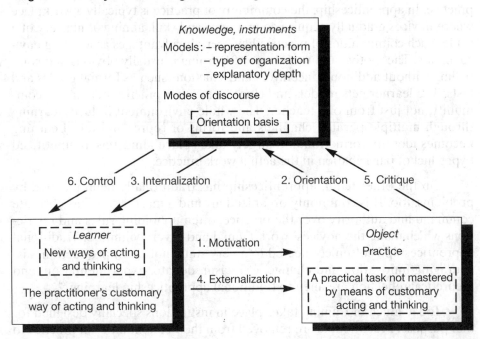

Earlier it was pointed out that substantial motivation, the first step in the cycle, represents the context of criticism in learning. Orientation and internalization, steps two and three, represent the context of discovery. In a similar vein, externalization (step 4) represents the *context of application.* Critique and control (steps 5 and 6) again represent the context of criticism. Each one of these contexts has its typical tools and modes of discourse. The context of criticism highlights the powers of questioning, contradicting and debating. The context of discovery highlights the powers of experimenting, modelling, symbolizing, and generalizing. The context of application highlights the powers of social relevance, community involvement, and guided practice. The integral learning cycle requires moving from one context to another, providing for complementary ways of knowing and thinking.[23]

Learning as community involvement

Up to now we have treated learning mainly from the point of view of one person and disregarded the social aspects of learning. Yet learning is always a series of social occurrences. Even when learning takes the form of individual study physically separated from other people, the application of what is studied will eventually happen in arenas of shared practice and social interaction.

Learning takes place either directly or indirectly in a community of practice. In apprenticeship, the community of practice is typically a workplace where novices gradually acquire competence and skill, aiming at mastery of a trade. Such communities of practice have certain advantages as learning environments. The motive and usefulness of learning is usually obvious and compelling without additional incentives and sanctions such as formal grades and tests. The learner gets models and clues from other practitioners in the community, not just from one teacher. The whole environment induces learning through multiple parallel channels and forms of representation. Learning becomes identity formation and largely takes place almost as an unnoticed byproduct of participation in the actual work practice.

On the other hand, apprenticeship has traditionally been plagued by problems, too. It is commonly organized around a master who has absolute command and authority over the practice, often upholding rules and restrictions which make the novices' work menial and severely limited. Traditional apprenticeship is often connected to a very static notion of production, discouraging innovation and change. Criticism, debate, experimentation, and theoretical reflection are alien to traditional apprenticeship learning.[24]

Today much of training takes place in institutions specially designed for that purpose. Practitioners are removed from their communities of practice to assure undisturbed and intensive learning. The paradox is that the very removal may also eliminate strong and rich sources and resources of learning – those discussed above as strengths of apprenticeship. Institutionalized training courses often suffer from the same problems described earlier in this chapter as weaknesses of school learning: textbooks and lecture contents tend to become objects in themselves, disconnected from the practices which eventually are supposed to be mastered.

Are we then stuck between two equally unsatisfactory alternatives: conservative apprenticeship learning in the workplace or traditional school-like text learning in training courses?

The alternatives may not in fact be so limited. Communities of investigative learning can be built both in workplaces and in institutionally organized training courses. These communities of investigative learning are typically *networks that cross and transcend boundaries between workplaces and training institutions.* Such transitional communities rely on a high degree of lateral interaction and communication between relatively autonomous teams.[25]

Learning as collaboration

It is common to keep the social factors of learning strictly apart from the cognitive factors. People are accustomed to thinking that intellectual instruction is given in lectures according to an exact schedule of organized courses, whereas group work, social skills, personal relations and joint activity are developed by using completely different styles of teaching. In adult education, various small group teaching models are used which generally do not emphasize the learning of new knowledge but concentrate instead on observing one's own and others' behaviour, on putting one's whole self into it and on making self-critical evaluations.[26]

The different training models certainly have their right to exist. But in the long run, it may be detrimental to completely separate cognitive and social factors. Situations might arise in which intellectual training is needlessly rudimentary and ineffective. Training aimed at social skills, however, might have a rather ostentatious effect unless cooperation, interaction and empathy are not linked up to the contents and mastering of some substantial tasks and practices. The separation of intellectual and social factors and the problems which result can be shown in the following example:

Most of the participants in the course follow the teaching carefully and work hard. However, the lecturers and director of the training session are bothered by the knowledge that one group of participants is living completely in its own separate experience.

This group carries on its own discussion which the others cannot follow. Sometimes it sounds as if it is related to the subject matter, at other times it seems remote. The members of the group sometimes laugh at something in the lecture which does not appear amusing to the others. At some moments they seem to completely lose interest in the teaching, but otherwise they perform their tasks independently and efficiently.

The director of the course feels the situation is a problem, but does not know quite what to do about it.

The emergence of this kind of "private culture" between students is completely normal. It always happens, even though in short courses it may not go further than preliminary contact and interaction between participants, and for that reason is not noticed by the course director and teachers.

The appearance of private social groupings is a symptom of a significant law of learning being neglected in instruction. The learning of mental performances which demand knowledge and skill begins at the point where the corresponding tasks are conducted externally, materially and *between people*. They are gradually *internalized* and become individual functions. Thus social interaction and joint work is the starting point of learning.[27] Indeed, it may be argued that the key difference between human learning and animal learning is the human capacity to learn from collaboration by means of taking simultaneously one's own and the partner's perspective.[28]

A growing number of studies indicate that the social interaction of students may have a decisive influence on the quality of learning.

This is clearly seen in experiments in which various tasks to be solved are given to students in pairs and in small groups.

Particularly at the stage in which a new idea or principle should be appropriated, it appears to be advantageous for learning to form pairs or small groups in which the knowledge, skills and concepts of the students vary. Tasks and problems are then given to the groups for reflection.

It may happen in such small groups that different students propose conflicting solutions to the same problem. They have differing concepts of the task and how to carry it out.

This *sociocognitive conflict* seems to be a very strong factor for promoting learning. The more able student has to account for and indicate concretely his or her point of view. Thus the student comes to understand it better him- or herself. The weaker student has to compare his or her perception with the opinions of the group partner. Through this conflict, the student discerns which one is the better alternative.

The successful outcome of this kind of conflict situation depends, of course, on how carefully prepared the task is. Conflict must not be left as an unfruitful, emotional dispute. The course of the task must be such that the different alternatives are tried in a pertinent way.

Students whose basic knowledge is weak have been observed to profit most from the use of such sociocognitive conflicts when learning a new concept or principle. It seems to even out the differences between the starting points of students.[29]

This example illustrates how the social factors of instruction can be intentionally made to serve the appropriation of a particular subject matter. When groups form themselves independently of any obvious cause, it is very often due to the fact that tasks included in the subject matter were not linked to social interaction between students. In such case, social interaction is sidetracked from the point of view of learning.

Traditional instruction basically aims at the improvement of the knowledge and skills of the individual. For this reason, it may even seem that studying is impossible to conduct in a genuine spirit of co-responsibility. However, this is not necessarily the case. Work-related adult training sessions are generally aimed at improving the mastery of actual practices, not merely at touching up an individual's knowledge and skills as such. Therefore the question is largely that of linking the learning of knowledge and skills to the development of actual joint work processes.

The instructor has the task of teaching the principles and methods needed by social workers in looking after various requests and instances of assistance. He knows that in reality, treating requests and solving situations are (or should be) a job which demands multi-professional teamwork.

He might, of course, teach the information and skills needed in this work in a way that each participant just studies "for oneself". This is perhaps the most common method. But done in this manner, a central factor and aspect of learning content remains untaught: the joint nature of the task.

The alternative method would include tasks in which participants must solve problems and apply the knowledge they learn in collaborative teams, similar to the situations of work practice. Internal division of labour and social-intellectual conflicts can be planned right into these tasks.

It has been shown that in a problem requiring the fashioning of a new orientation basis, the externalization of already acquired principles, or creative application, there is often an advantage in letting participants discuss their interpretation of the task and proposals to solve it in pairs or small groups.

At the signal of an alarm, supervisors of automated production processes must identify the problem and select the right procedure for correcting it in an often complicated order which involves numerous factors of uncertainty. An employee acting alone in this case easily holds on to the one solution he or she supposes to be correct and repeats it persistently, even when it does not lead to the desired result (the so-called tunnel effect). This narrowing down of thinking may be overcome by letting another or several other employees search for the solution to the same problem and critically compare the proposed alternatives.

Through studies a person not only appropriates subject matter, but study habits as well, often without noticing.

Study skills are the individual's ability to master his or her own learning process. A skilled student consciously monitors his or her own work: motivates and orientates him- or herself, internalizes new material, externalizes it and willfully controls his or her learning. This kind of developed learning skill is difficult to acquire. For example, motivation and orientation are mental actions which are not at all easy.

Above it was pointed out that mental actions first appear in external and material form and between people. They are internalized as they gradually start taking place in the individual's mind. The same applies to learning skills.

The appropriation of learning skills along with learning content can be significantly improved by utilizing social interaction between students. In this case, motivation can be accomplished as *collective* motivation, orientation as *collective* orientation, etc. Students then motivate and orientate each other in a community of investigative learning.

Instead of each student solving a separate, motivational problem and cognitive conflict, the same task could be given to a groups of students.

Instead of formulating the orientation basis for a new subject by way of individual student responses, pairs or small groups could be asked to search for a general model of explanation, an orientation basis which fits the problems presented.

Instead of the instructor transmitting the subject matter, he or she can let pairs of students or small groups go through the key issues of the lesson amongst themselves. A conversation which outlines and systematizes the subject often succeeds better if students have first had the chance in pairs or groups to search out the unclear areas and important correlations of a subject.

The same applies to externalization. In task performance, group work has been traditionally recommended. Often it is particularly effective to first let students solve some of the questions together and after that switch to the individual performance of tasks which are based on the same principles.

What of the control of learning? Why should the instructor always control students' comprehension? Students can do it themselves by interrogating one another, correcting each others' work and checking each others' understanding. This is an effective manner of learning self-monitoring.

Three types of collaboration

There are different types of collaboration which yield different results from the viewpoint of learning. We differentiate between three types: coordination, cooperation, and communication.[30]

Coordination refers to situations where each student focuses on his or her specific part of a common task without reflecting jointly on the task as a whole. The rules and division of labour are determined by the teacher who also has the overall view of the whole task. The students interact mainly to smooth out boundaries and overlaps between their sub-tasks. Thus, their interaction has a somewhat routine and externally regulated character. The learning outcomes are mainly individual skills and insights, although combined they form a meaningful larger pattern.

Cooperation refers to situations in which the students focus on a shared task or problem, trying to find mutually acceptable ways to conceptualize and solve it. The students are not any more confined to predetermined individual sub-tasks and roles. They exchange ideas and roles intensively in order to master the task together. Thus, the division of labour as well as the rules for work are modified and reconstructed in the very process of cooperation. However, the students do not jointly reflect on their own interaction; it remains improvised. The learning outcomes are typically shared innovative models and tools for solving given tasks.

Finally *communication* refers to situations where the students not only focus on a shared task but also on the rules and division of labour of their own interaction. Thus, the interaction gains a reflective character, developing over a longer period of time. The learning outcomes of such reflective communication are not restricted to models for solving given problems; the students also learn new ways and means of working together.

A full-blown model of investigative learning

Social interaction and collaborative work oblige us once again to elaborate further the model of investigative learning. We must add three components to the model presented in diagram 7, namely *learning community, rules*, and *division of labour.*

Learning community refers to the group of learners and instructors who share the same objects of learning. As was mentioned above, in investigative learning the community is not restricted to a classroom. More typically it takes the form of a network of learning that connects teams in workplaces and institutions that provide systematic training.

Rules refer to given or negotiated guidelines, directives, scripts and plans that regulate the learning process. In traditional school learning, the official syllabus usually determines the pace and contents of work, commonly by specifying the textbook chapters to be taught and studied within given periods of time. Additional rules typically focus on grading and external student behaviour. In investigative learning rules are different, typically criteria of productive inquiry and valid argument or insight. Curricula are used as tools rather than as externally given rules (see Chapter 7).

Division of labour refers to how tasks and roles are distributed among students and teachers. In traditional school learning, the dominant division of labour is such that the teacher lectures and the students listen and take notes,

Diagram 8: A full-blown model of investigative learning

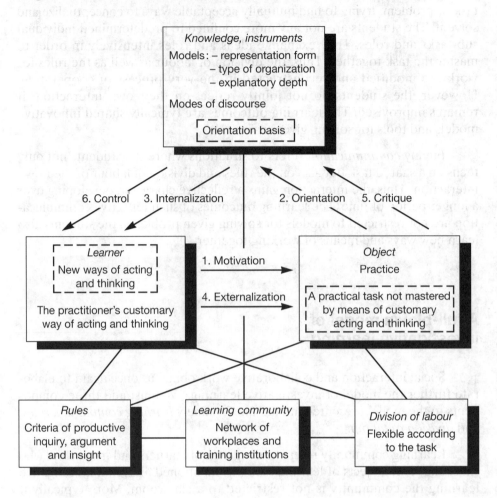

or the teacher gives and controls assignments and the students work on them individually. In investigative learning, the division of labour is flexibly altered according to the nature of the task and the step in the learning cycle.

A full-blown model of investigative learning is presented in diagram 8. The model calls for serious attention to the social aspect of learning while retaining the integral cycle as the core of investigative learning.

From investigative to expansive learning in work practice

We have now outlined four conditions for investigative deep-level learning:

o   substantial motivation, launched by the utilization of a cognitive (or sociocognitive) conflict;

o   organization of learning contents by means of models and modes of discourse, employing multiple forms of representation;

o   an integral learning cycle, comprised of the six steps of motivation, orientation, internalization, externalization, critique, and control;

o   networks of learning and multiple types of collaborative learning.

Even simple skills are better learnt – they become more flexible – when the learner understands the principles behind them. It is therefore incorrect to imagine that mechanical work tasks would be most economically taught by simple demonstration and repetition. The models thus formed are narrow and their application potential is restricted. An employee taught in this manner and met with a problem which takes him or her by surprise is often in a predicament, either being mentally paralysed or acting rashly and making mistakes. Without understanding the principles of the task, it is difficult to resiliently and innovatively develop a functioning solution to a novel problem. When problems are understood, on the other hand, it is possible that practitioners not only solve them but also predict and prevent them.

Descriptive, superficial information generally supports a person's conventional ideas and prejudices. It may therefore be considered as being "value-free" and neutral. Inquiry into the causes, origins and principles of phenomena requires that learners take stands, form value judgements, and envision desirable futures.

These characteristics of investigative learning indicate that such learning often opens up possibilities of change and development in communities of practice. We speak of *expansive learning*, or third order learning, when a community of practice begins to analyse and transform itself. Such expansive learning is not any more limited to pre-defined contents and tasks. Rather, it is a long-term process of re-defining the objects, tools and social structures of the workplace. While expansive learning is not the main focus of this book, it is important to realize that instruction which elicits investigative learning remains a vital instrument in such large-scale processes of change.[31]

Earlier in this chapter we used the example of training factory inspectors (see page 28). Expansive learning in this domain would first of all require that the practitioners and trainers analyse the historical evolution of the work of factory inspectors' work and orientations. Such an analysis could lead to

---

Diagram 9: A collective zone of proximal development for factory inspectors[32]

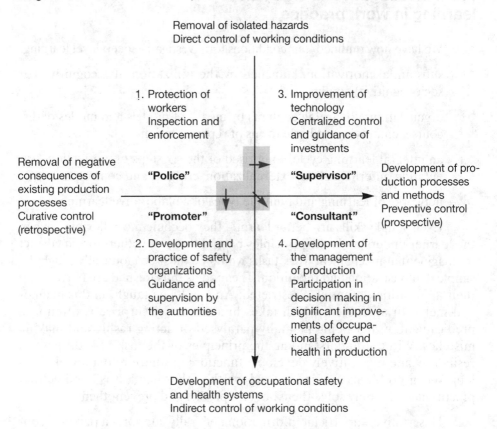

Removal of isolated hazards
Direct control of working conditions

1. Protection of workers Inspection and enforcement

3. Improvement of technology Centralized control and guidance of investments

Removal of negative consequences of existing production processes
Curative control (retrospective)

"Police"

"Supervisor"

"Promoter"

"Consultant"

Development of production processes and methods
Preventive control (prospective)

2. Development and practice of safety organizations Guidance and supervision by the authorities

4. Development of the management of production Participation in decision making in significant improvements of occupational safety and health in production

Development of occupational safety and health systems
Indirect control of working conditions

the identification of the current *collective zone of proximal development* in that community of practice. The zone is a contested area between the traditional practice and alternative future directions.

In diagram 9, a zone of proximal development for factory inspectors work is sketched by means of two dimensions. The horizontal dimension represents change from retrospective, curative control toward preventive development of production processes. The vertical dimension represents change from direct control of hazards toward indirect control by means of developing occupational safety and health (OSH) systems in workplaces. The two dimensions yield four fields which represent alternative historical orientation types: "police", "promoter", "supervisor", and "consultant". The zone of intensive learning and innovation is marked as a gray wave moving away from the traditional "police"-like work of inspectors.

Expansive learning is collective construction of the future for a community of practice. It involves creating visions like diagram 9 and also turning those visions into practical action.

[1] For extended analysis and empirical research on people's conceptions of learning, see Säljö (1982).

[2] For studies of collective memory, see the volume edited by Middleton & Edwards (1990).

[3] On levels of learning, see the pioneering work of Bateson (1972) and the further elaboration in Engeström (1987).

[4] A classical critique of traditional school learning may be found in Whitehead (1929). Becker's (1972) article is a powerful statement of the same dilemma. Freire's work (1988) contains another important version of the critique. For recent cognitive analyses, see Resnick (1987b) and Gardner (1990).

[5] See Marton, Hounsell & Entwistle (1984).

[6] Entwistle (1981) distinguishes between the anxious type motivated by the fear of failure and the self-assured type motivated by a goal of success. The latter can often effectively use different study techniques, even though the interest lies outside the subject matter.

[7] Pioneering work in this direction was done by Berlyne (1960). Lind (1975) offers a good summary of early research related to substantial learning motivation. In activity theory, studies by Bratus (1990) and Hakkarainen (1988) are particularly useful.

[8] Dilemmas are analysed by Billig et al. (1988).

[9] This triadic division was set forward by Jerome Bruner (1966); he used the terms enactive, iconic and symbolic for the forms of representation.

[10] For analysis of gestures, see McNeill (1992). For studies on metaphors, see Ortony (1979) and Lakoff & Johnson (1980). For analysis of narrative, see Bruner (1990). For studies on the potentials of new media for learning, see Greenfield (1984); Harel & Papert (1991); Papert (1980); and Salomon (1981).

[11] See Gentner & Stevens (1983).

[12] This emerging new approach to models is captured in Rogers, Rutherford & Bibby (1992).

[13] See Bruner (1963), pp. 31-32.

[14] This example is based on ideas developed for an ILO course for African factory inspectors in 1992; see also Virkkunen (1991) and Vähäpassi (1992). Both examples will be elaborated further in Chapter 4.

[15] See Schön (1983) and Zuboff (1988).

[16] See Harré (1992).

[17] The concepts of "social language" and "speech genre" were originally developed by Bakhtin (1981; 1986); an accessible discussion of these is provided by Wertsch (1991). A good introduction to the analysis of discourse can be found in Potter and Wetherell (1987). On the relationship between mental models and discourse, see Garnham (1987).

[18] Mills (1967), pp. 441-442.

[19] For analysis of argumentation as a mode of thought and discourse, see Billig (1987).

[20] See Davydov (1988). There are other models of learning cycles, notably that of Kolb (1984). Kolb's cycle depicts learning exclusively as an experiential process, whereas the model presented here sees productive learning as interplay between experience and theoretical reflection. Theoretical models are formed by analysing both practical experience and conceptual materials, such as texts.

[21] Steps 5 and 6 are particularly important for the development of the learner's self-reflection and so called metacognitive skills. On metacognition, see Forrest-Pressley, MacKinnon & Waller (1985); Nelson (1992); Reeve & Brown (1984); Sheinker & Sheinker (1989); Weinert & Kluwe (1987).

[22] This model is elaborated in Engeström, Hakkarainen & Hedegaard (1984).

[23] See Eisner (1985) and Gardner (1983).

[24] See Lave & Wenger (1991) and Rorabaugh (1986) for different accounts of apprenticeship.

[25] For a discussion of network organizations, see Powell (1990). Examples of networks of investigative learning are given by Moll & Greenberg (1990) and Sutter & Grensjö (1988).

[26] The ideas of Carl Rogers (1969; 1970) are an influential source of these models.

[27] This law was put forward by the Russian psychologist L. S. Vygotsky in the 1920s; his work became well known in the west only in the 1970s (see Vygotsky, 1978).

[28] See Tomasello, Kruger & Ratner (1992).

[29] On sociocognitive conflict, see Perret-Clermont (1980); Smith, Johnson & Johnson (1981); Ames & Murray (1982); Perret-Clermont & Brossard (1985). For recent studies and experiences of collaborative learning in general, see Brubacher, Payne & Rickett (1990); Clarke, Wideman & Eadie (1990); Cohen (1986); Davidson & Worsham (1992); Johnson & Johnson (1989); Kagan (1989); Sharan (1990); and Slavin (1990).

[30] See Raeithel (1983); Fichtner (1984); and Engeström (1992).

[31] See Engeström (1987) and Engeström (1991a) for discussions and examples of expansive learning.

[32] This diagram is a modified version of earlier models presented by Virkkunen (1991) and Vähäpassi (1992).

WHAT IS GOOD INSTRUCTION?

3

Learning and instruction

In the first two chapters, we sketched a conception of human learning based on cognitive psychology and activity theory. But what is the relationship between learning and instruction? They are not the same thing. Plenty of learning goes on without instruction, nor does all instruction necessarily lead to the kind of learning hoped for.

Learning is an activity of the student, whereas instruction is an activity of the teacher. The purpose of teaching, or of the instructional process, is to intertwine these two activities as much as possible. They never fall fully into one strand: the student always learns to some extent in a manner not intended by the teacher. The ongoing tension and excitement lies exactly in the fact that instruction is not merely transmission, pouring knowledge into empty bowls.

> The instructor is trying to establish a classroom discussion, and a student stands up and asks a question that doesn't make sense or that seems obviously shallow and uncomprehending. Classroom discussion is a fragile power. "Dumb" questions test an instructor's mind and intentions. Students watch to see how the instructor will respond, and the instructor knows they do. He wants to give a question the weight it deserves, but he doesn't want to cut the questioner down. So he probes, leading the student into discussion, trying to move from the original question toward other questions that are more worth discussion, more answerable, or both. Sometimes the instructor discovers what the student had in mind in the first place. Sometimes the instructor and the questioner together find a reasonable question that can be addressed and answered with dignity and intellectual profit to both sides.
>
> The instructor and the student have engaged for a short time in an indeterminate discourse. Maintaining conversation, they have sought a common ground of comprehension and understanding. For a few moments, the instructor has established what Vygotsky calls a zone of proximal development and what Newman, Griffin, and Cole call the construction zone. The construction zone mediates between the thought of two people. It is a shared activity in which interpsychological processes can take place.[1]

Here the zone of proximal development, or the construction zone, refers to micro-level processes between learners and instructors.[2] The crucial point is that the instructor has a responsibility for creating such zones.

Although there are many occasions of productive learning in everyday situations, most of everyday learning consists of conditioning, imitation, and trial and error. Investigative, deep-level learning is relatively rare without instruction or intentional self-instruction. For that very reason, instruction is necessary. Its task is to enhance the quality of learning, to make it purposeful and methodical.

In teaching, the instructor directs the students' learning efforts. The instructor's work is aimed at purposeful and integral learning. He or she organizes conflicts leading to substantial learning motivation. For the student, this means intellectual confrontations, challenges and demands. On the other hand, the instructor also guides and assists the students through cycles of investigative learning.

Good instruction strides ahead of learning and paves the way for learning. Under the guidance of a good teacher, students become more independent. Consciousness of and responsibility for their own learning increase.

Moving through the steps of an integral learning cycle, the teacher's role changes. At the outset, the teacher challenges the students, as if playing the role of a "devil's advocate" in order to create a motivating cognitive conflict. Next, the teacher invites the students to experiment and draft models, providing materials and tools. When the students begin to operate with their newly formulated models or orientation bases, the teacher offers them further knowledge. In the practical application of the new models, the teacher adopts the viewpoint of competent practitioner, demanding solutions to real-life problems and situations.

Thus, teaching is much more than merely a presentation to the public or spontaneous interaction with students. It involves:

o   *organizing* the contexts and communities of learning;

o   *formulating* instructional objectives;

o   *structuring* instructional contents;

o   *guiding and monitoring* the students' advancement through the integral cycle of investigative learning;

o   *interacting and conducting conversation* with the students;

o   *planning and assessing* the overall instructional process.

In the following chapters, we will discuss the tasks listed above, starting from the formulation of instructional objectives (Chapter 3). Before that, we will briefly delineate the first task in the list, namely that of organizing the contexts and communities of learning.

Teaching as organizing

Teaching always takes place in an intellectual and organizational context. In Chapter 2, we sketched three kinds of *intellectual contexts*: the context of criticism, the context of discovery, and the context of application. Each one of these intellectual contexts requires its own typical tools, materials and modes of discourse.

We also pointed out that the *organizational context* that seems most fruitful for investigative learning is a network of relatively autonomous teams that transcend the boundaries between training institutions and workplaces.

Instructors often feel that the context of their work is given from above. This feeling of powerlessness is tied to the tradition of working alone. In order to change and modify their contexts of learning and teaching, instructors need to work together and seek allies outside their immediate institutional settings. Such network building empowers instructors and enhances learning.

In Finland, the primary health care system needs to be reorganized to respond better to the changing needs of clients. To accomplish this, a project called "The Working Health Centre" was started in 1990. Twenty local health centres from different parts of the country formed a network, and each health centre is reorganizing itself by forming relatively autonomous multiprofessional teams. All this was supported and stimulated by training and guidance given by a national project group. The training was not limited to isolated courses. It became a tool in the wider context of changing the practice. Much of the training was given in local workplaces, while part of it was given centrally in special training facilities. Investigative learning was not limited to training sessions but was conducted as an integral part of the everyday practice in many health centres. All this was stimulated by continuous exchange of experiences, ideas and results between the participating health centres and their teams.

There are numerous examples of learning networks organized by means of telecommunications technology. In such networks of learning, classrooms and other sites of learning often interact across great geographic distances and cultural barriers.[3]

The principles of instruction

Every training session and educational organization has its own instructional particularities. Teaching always expresses some principles, general concepts about learning and teaching, whether they be conscious or not.

The viewpoints which lie behind a given instruction are often neither recognized nor publicly stated. For that reason, teaching contains some "hidden principles". Sometimes beautifully expressed fundamental ideas are in conflict with the hidden principles brought out by practical experience.

Instructional principles are the general viewpoints about learning and teaching on which instruction is built. Besides being hidden or openly stated, they might be consistent or in conflict with each other. Training sessions are often internally incoherent because the instructional principles they observe have not been well thought out. Each instructor acts according to his or her own preferences and instincts.

The trainee often gets the impression that the most important instructional principle of training was indifference on the part of the planners with regards to trainees and the quality of learning. This might be called the hidden principle of intellectual laziness or also the principle of a detached administrative attitude.

When one begins to define the principles to be proclaimed, one must bear in mind two starting points: first, one's concept or theory of learning and teaching; second, one's concept of the objectives and purposes of the particular instruction in question. Instructional principles can be understood as a guide by which the teacher and students utilize the teaching-learning process for accomplishing chosen objectives.

We cannot present, then, any universal or impartial list of instructional principles. In a sense, the instructional principles are the programme manifesto of each instructional corpus or training course. Their task is to give to teachers and students a crystallized overview of the theory, objectives and use of instructional means. In a curriculum or syllabus, the instructional principles are often expressed in the form of a concise description of the methods or styles of work to be observed.

The general instructional principles proposed in this book can be found in condensed form at the end of the book in the section "Golden rules of teaching". It is worthwhile to seriously consider what kind of instructional principles should be raised in training in a community of practice. At times it might also be useful to ask students how they would characterize the principles of the teaching they have received. This may reveal gaps and conflicts between what was declared and the hidden principles actually experienced by the students.

---

[1] White (1989), p. xi. Views of teaching similar to the one advocated in this book have been recently put forward by Moll (1990); Newman, Griffin & Cole (1989); and Tharp & Gallimore (1988). However, this book puts more emphasis on the formation of theoretical concepts and theoretical thinking in instruction, inspired by the work of Davydov (1988; 1990); see also Hedegaard, Hakkarainen & Engeström (1984) and Markova (1979).

[2] When we discussed expansive learning at the end of Chapter 2, the zone of proximal development was used to characterize change of work practices at a collective and historical level.

[3] See Kay (1991); Kearsley (1985); Riel & Levin (1990); Roberts et al. (1990).

FORMULATING COGNITIVE OBJECTIVES OF INSTRUCTION

4

Why are instructional objectives necessary?

The usual answer to this question is that:

Objectives are needed so that instructors, employers and students know what trainees should be capable of after training.

This is of course correct, but at the same time superficial. Such an idea of the purpose of teaching objectives limits teaching to external factors. Diagram 10 restates this book's view of teaching. Instructional objectives, the focus of this chapter, are highlighted in italics.

The reader should consider the following question:

Why are instructional objectives needed from the point of view of the internal factors of instruction, i.e. with the cognitive activity of students in mind?

It may be concluded that objectives based on the internal factors of instruction present above all an attempt to help students study consciously and seriously; to keep them constantly aware of the whole and overall principle to which each moment's activity is linked. On this basis, we may define the function of an instructional objective as follows:

The purpose of an instructional objective is to direct the students' efforts to the most essential principles and to the overall structure of the subject matter.

Behavioural objectives do not suffice

Below is an example of objectives which were set for a course organized by a certain government institution:

Initiation Course

A. Overall objective

to give a general picture of state administration and this institution; to explain the rights and duties of those being trained; to create a basis for developing a correct attitude and desire for cooperation.

B. Specific objectives

1) Knowledge: After the initiation course, the trainee should possess a general picture, mainly from the point of view of his or her own unit, of

○ work duties and regulations in this institution;

○ the administration, tasks and organization of the institution;

○ personnel matters;

Diagram 10: The external and internal factors in teaching (2)

External factors (means by which students' observable behaviour and situation are controlled)	Internal factors (means by which students' mental work is guided)
Instructional objectives	
desired observable performances described in the form of behavioural objectives	contents to be mastered, described in the form of cognitive objectives, or orientation bases of performances
Study motivation	
stimuli, rewards and punishments to keep the attention of the students	students' interest in the subject matter awakened through intellectual confrontation and cognitive conflict
Choice of teaching content	
ready-made facts and performance schemes	models, principles, systems of ideas, and modes of discourse
Methods of teaching	
variable forms of teaching; entertainment; maintenance of momentary alertness; assurance of students' external activeness	stepwise realization of an entire cycle of learning by means of complete instructional treatment
Output of planning	
time schedule, lecture outline, transparencies	curriculum for a thematic unit of instruction, explaining the progress of teaching from the viewpoint of learning
The instructor in the teaching situation (teaching skills)	
presentation skills; command of immediate social interaction; organizational skills; audiovisual techniques	command of the content of the subject matter; flexible reliance on the curriculum; instructor's ethics

2) Skills: The student should possess

o sufficient skills to perform his or her own work tasks and to further develop them.

3) Attitudes: The student should

o possess an affirmative attitude towards his or her own work and the institution;

o agree with the institution's aims.

This is a fairly typical list of so-called behavioural objectives of instruction.[1] What purpose do they serve?

Obviously useful from the point of view of employers or supervisors, these objectives give a rough idea of what can be expected from people who have gone through the course and how they might perform in an organization. At the same time, they serve the participants themselves by giving them an outline of what they will be capable of after the course.

Such objectives, consequently, serve primarily administrative purposes. But from the perspective of teaching and learning, their functions remain external factors. The objective is not really helping the student to learn better, nor the instructor to teach better. That is to say, the learner and the teacher do not find in behavioural objectives essential principles and overall constructs of the subject matter. In fact they find practically nothing about the contents of instruction and learning in behavioural objectives.

The objectives listed above state that by the time the course is over, the trainees will have acquired a general picture of their institution. But what are the essential features of that general picture? What are its contents and structure?

Let us look at another example, this time concerning objectives of a course on customer service in banking.

At the end of the course, trainees should

o be familiar with the types of bank accounts and the possibilities of holding them;

o be able to record entries in a savings account;

o be able to clear withdrawals from a savings account;

o know the proceedings for closing a savings account and opening a new one.

Is this not exact and concrete enough? Shouldn't this kind of objective be a good enough guide for learning and teaching?

Let us analyse the objective a little further.

First, what is meant by the expression "be familiar with the types of bank accounts and the possibilities of holding them"? The trainee probably should know the names of the various accounts and the differences between them. But on what is this knowledge based? The ability to name and recognize accounts might be based on "fixed" facts, lists which have been memorized. *Or else*, understanding the origin and principles of the different accounts could be the basis for performance, in which case the trainee recognizes why there are different kinds of accounts.

Next, what is meant by the words "be able to record entries in a savings account"? Seemingly, this means that at the end of the course the trainee should know the practical steps of correctly entering a deposit in a savings account by means of punching and saving it into a computerized database. With practice, these tasks can be learned as automatic motor reflexes. *Or else* learning the task could be based on understanding *why* the entry is marked in a certain way and at a certain place in the computer system. In the latter case, understanding the origin and principles of the bank's information system forms the basis of knowing how to perform. Otherwise stated, the trainee understands the banking system of keeping accounts as a whole, created to meet certain needs of individuals and businesses.

If a participant learns to understand the principles, performance will not be only a stiff routine. The principles are tools of thought on which one can fall back in unforeseen problem situations where routines do not work.

If the learning of principles is to be promoted, it is not good enough to list externally fixed performances as objectives, or to name and describe desired behavioural outcomes. At best, such objectives serve administrative purposes. At worst, they become a formal exercise designed to make the course description look more impressive and "exact".

The same external performances can be based on completely different internal models and cognitive constructs. For example, the bank clerk's habitual, everyday operations can be learned either "the hard way" or on the basis of understanding the principles of the system of accounts. From the outside, performance seems the same. The value of a deeper cognitive construct is only revealed in a crisis situation in which the employee is called upon to solve an unexpected problem independently.

If the objective only describes fixed, external performance, teaching and learning will likely be planned so as to lead as directly as possible to that performance. The internal conditions of external performance will be disregarded. The internal models and cognitive constructs will therefore emerge as if in the dark, easily remaining narrow and superficial.

Manuals for formulating behavioural objectives stress that only well bounded observable behaviours shall be named in such objectives. Take the example of a hockey team. The coach tries to teach the team to play well.

When only observable behaviours are acceptable objectives, the natural tendency is to emphasize the physical performance. The focus is fixed on specific external skills, moves, and manoeuvres. Such aspects of the game as diagnosing the opponent's tactics or analyzing and weighing alternative strategies for one's own team are definitely not observable behaviours – they are crucial aspects of the "inner game".[2] If one tries to translate them into discrete observable behaviours – such as "name and define five typical strategies used by hockey teams" – one destroys their essential character as processes relying on holistic patterns and models.

Manuals for writing behavioural objectives emphasize that each desired performance must be specified and taught to the student separately. Thus, lists of behavioural objectives for a domain of knowledge and skill tend to become very voluminous. The possibility of acquiring fewer, more powerful cognitive tools and models that can be used to generate appropriate performances across many situations is overlooked. This leads to assembly line-like rigidity and overloading in instruction. If such instruction and training dominates, people, especially those employed in jobs which change constantly and entail unpredictable situations, are put in serious jeopardy.

Formulating cognitive objectives

From the point of view of learning, it is important to *substantially describe in the objectives those principles and constructs on the understanding of which external performances are to be built*. The "red thread" and gist of the subject matter – what insight is to be attained through a course – should be discovered already at the beginning.

Going beyond the desired external behaviours, *cognitive objectives describe models which can be used as tools for generating and monitoring appropriate performances in changing conditions*. Such models are formulated primarily by asking why a certain performance is successful and how did it originate.

Example 1

Earlier we described the alternative ways of teaching the use of an internal-combustion engine.

The behavioural objective of this kind of instruction could be: "At the end of the course, students will be able to name and recognize the important parts of the internal-combustion engine, turn it on, regulate its speed and turn it off."

These external performances can be learnt without understanding the active principle of the motor. But the person who only knows the motor in this manner will be in a dilemma the day it malfunctions or a new model of it is taken into use.

The formulation of a cognitive objective means that one asks why the motor has exactly those parts, why it is turned on in exactly this way.

One answers these questions by explaining the motor's origination. It concerns the utilization of heat: the heat released from burning fuel is transformed into compressed energy, which is converted into mechanical work. This starting point is common to the internal-combustion engine and the steam engine. But the internal-combustion engine is a step ahead of the steam engine because in the steam engine the conversion of energy takes place by degrees so that energy is lost, while in the internal-combustion engine, the conversion of energy happens in one chamber (in the cylinder) and very quickly, as explosion-like combustion.

From here it is easy for the instructor to continue, carefully describing the functional principle of the combustion engine and after that, the functions of the various parts of the motor.

Example 2

Our second example again concerns the training of new factory inspectors.

The behavioural objective of such a course could be as follows: "The student will be able to identify and name the important steps of a factory inspection and perform those steps in the correct order in realistic practice situations."

The inspectors can indeed be taught to memorize and perform the steps of a standard inspection procedure by means of repetition and reinforcement. The problem is that such a standard procedure has to be continuously modified and sometimes changed radically in order to cope with different workplace conditions and situations. When the standard procedure is taught as such, without questioning its origins and principles, the necessary modifications and changes in practical situations are left at the mercy of the individual inspector's improvization.

The formulation of cognitive objectives would mean that one asks why the standard inspection procedure is just like it is, what are its origins and principles. This opens up an entirely different level of thinking. It becomes apparent that there is not just one universally applicable standard procedure but several alternative types that correspond to the more general historical orientation types of inspectors' work sketched in diagram 9 at the end of Chapter 2. Each procedure is an embodiment of certain historically changing principles and values.

By formulating cognitive objectives, then, one intends to expose the heart of the subject matter in order to know what kind of a model one wants the students to acquire. Exposing the heart of the matter is laborious. It requires thorough mastery of the subject matter contents. Such mastery of the contents is more than knowledge of what is said in textbooks; it requires insight into the interplay between theory and practice.

Orientation basis [3]

The model that a person uses to fashion his or her own understanding of something, to evaluate it and to solve tasks connected with it is called *orientation basis*.

Imagine that ten people are asked to sketch the ground plan of a railway station they all know. The result will be ten different diagrams. If a person had never been to the station, his or her drawing would probably be the one which deviated most from reality. In this respect he or she has a weaker orientation basis than the others.

Yet the others obviously also have fairly hazy and mistaken ideas of the train station. The weakness of each one's orientation basis would be further exposed if they were asked to mark on their drawings the most important procedures to be followed in the event of fire in a given part of the building. Specialists would find the drawings quite inadequate as an aid for functioning effectively and productively. Obviously the people who drew the diagrams were not well informed about the functional and structural principles of the station.

This is natural. In an area which is not directly connected with his or her professional competence or hobbies, a person mainly functions according to rather vague models and implicit everyday experience.

But what if one has as trainees station officials whose duties include security in case of accidents? In this case, an insufficient, haphazard orientation based on tacit experience is not good enough. Officials must be aware of the structure of the station and of how it functions; they must form an orientation basis on which to act quickly and successfully in any number of surprising situations.

This presupposes that the instructor is able to bring out those principles and to build out of them an explanatory model as a basis for instruction. In order to discover the principles, he or she must trace the source of the subject being taught. What did the architect have in mind when he or she designed the station building? What tasks, objectives and problems was his or her design meant to solve? What principles guided the design? What practical forces have modified those principles and how? By answering these questions, the instructor can shape a simplified model of the functional idea of the station.

The orientation basis is reconstructed several times in the instructional process. First it is prepared beforehand by the instructor. Next it takes shape in the beginning stages of instruction by means of collaborative analysis and experimentation - which can significantly transform the model from the form initially prepared by the instructor. Then the orientation basis is gradually internalized, which again involves transformations. Finally, when the model is applied in practical tasks, it will also be criticized and possibly improved.

At first the orientation basis is sketched on paper or represented in external form by other means, including discussion and debate between the students and instructors. It is gradually internalized and represented mentally.

A clear, graphic model can be a significant help in learning complex ideas and performances. It gives the student a framework or lens with which to interpret, organize and apply the material he or she is appropriating.

Imagine what it would be like to be given a book to read from which the cover, title page, list of contents and foreword have been ripped out. To start reading would be certainly dismaying. It would be difficult to situate the book, to identify what one is reading and how to analyse it.[4]

The title, the table of contents and the foreword offer an initial orientation to the contents of a book. But they are rarely very sophisticated as orientation bases. A table of contents does not usually reveal the crucial principles or ideas of the text. Being a linear list, it can hardly show the dynamic interconnections of the different themes of the book.

A good orientation basis does the following:

o   It gives a clear, systematic overall picture of the substance to be learned, thus helping the student to focus on a meaningful pattern or structure rather than on a mass of isolated details.

o   It helps the student to perform tasks, functioning as an external support and tool that can gradually be internalized.

o   Crystallizing the most salient and important features of the contents to be learned, the orientation basis also helps the student to question and criticize the validity of those contents, as well as to control, evaluate and correct his or her own performance.

An orientation basis can be expressed and represented in multiple ways and modalities. It is important that students do not become fixated on one single model which they regard as the only "correct" representation of a phenomenon. Flexible transformations and modifications are important when working with orientation bases.

For example in the orientation basis of the internal-combustion engine, it might not be enough to designate the functional principle of the motor as the conversion of heat into compressed energy and then into mechanical work by utilizing explosion-like combustion in one chamber.

In the first place, this principle stems from the problem it solved, the defects of the steam engine being poor efficiency and large loss of energy. Secondly, the principle should be linked to practice. One should explain how it is applied to the actual internal-combustion engine (through the cylinder, the piston, the fuel product, the ignition, the combustion chamber, the movement of the piston, the driving piston rod, etc.). These things can often be explained with the help of a diagram, or series of complementary diagrams.

A good orientation basis stimulates the independent development and derivation of further complementary orientation bases which illuminate different aspects or parts of a whole. A student who has internalized the general principle of the internal-combustion engine and the related functions of the different parts of the motor may produce independently a more specific model required for starting the motor.

An orientation basis can be presented in many ways. A simplified outline or model diagram filled out with text is often very effective. One could also use a series of orienting questions, directions or flow charts (algorithms) which help to perform tasks or solve problems in the given area.

This book, for example, has two overarching orientation bases. The first orientation basis is presented in diagram 1 in the section "This guidebook's view of teaching". Its principle is the distinction and correlation between internal and external factors. A simplified model is provided, depicting steps followed in the planning of instruction. The second orientation basis is developed in a stepwise manner in diagrams 2, 3, 4, 6, 7, and 8. Diagram 8 depicts a full-blown model of investigative learning which is the core orientation basis for the acquisition and application of this book's ideas.

Example 1: Orientation bases for mastering a motor

What kind of orientation basis, or series of complementary orientation bases, could be drawn for instructing the use of an internal-combustion engine?

The origin of the engine has been outlined above: the conversion by detonation of the energy contained in fuel into compressed energy and then into mechanical work.

This principle can be made concrete in a diagram such as the following:

Diagram 11: The basic structure of an internal-combustion engine

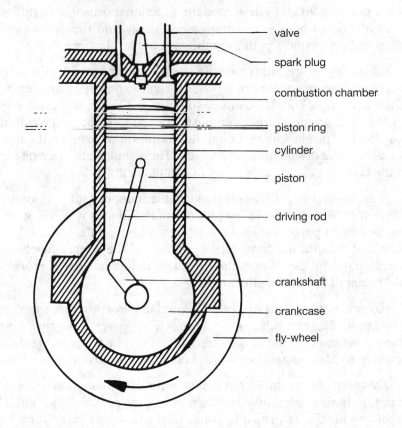

- valve
- spark plug
- combustion chamber
- piston ring
- cylinder
- piston
- driving rod
- crankshaft
- crankcase
- fly-wheel

The special parts of the internal-combustion engine are shown in connection with the diagram:

1) the cylinder block and crankcase

2) the cylinder head

3) the crank mechanism (the crankshaft and the fly-wheel, the driving rod, the piston and piston pin)

4) the valve mechanism (the camshaft, the valve lifters, the valves and springs).

Besides these basic parts, the continuous functioning of the motor requires a host of other things: a lubrication system, a fuelling system, a cooling system and an igniting apparatus.

The model given in diagram 11 is static; it does not tell what moves and how when the engine functions. From the standpoint of the dynamic functional principle, the practical importance of the motor's parts is explained when the diagram is completed as follows:

Diagram 12: The functional principle of the internal-combustion engine

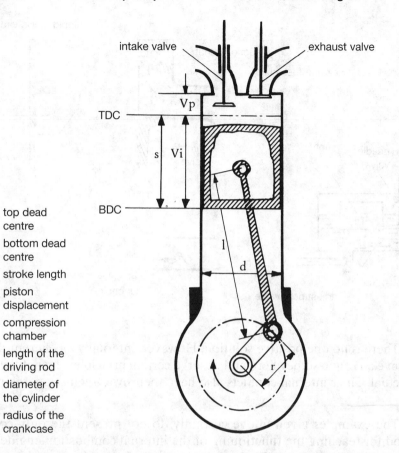

TDC	top dead centre
BDC	bottom dead centre
s	stroke length
Vi	piston displacement
Vp	compression chamber
l	length of the driving rod
d	diameter of the cylinder
r	radius of the crankcase

With the help of this diagram, the functional principle of the motor can be specified as a concrete series of occurrences divided into a certain number of stages.

From here we can move on to the functioning of four- and two-stroke cycle motors and so on.

On the basis of this kind of general orientation, as studies advance students can more and more independently construct orientation bases for various separate points within the whole field. For example, the functioning of the carburettor might be represented as shown on p. 62.

Of course, a problem in practical training is that not nearly all topics can be as clearly analysed and perfectly mastered as the internal-combustion engine. Legislation, for instance, may contain many inconsistencies. It does not even necessarily "have to work" as does the engine. How then does one draw an orientation basis for a subject which is substantially incoherent and scantily researched?

Diagram 13: The functional principle of the carburettor of an internal-combustion engine

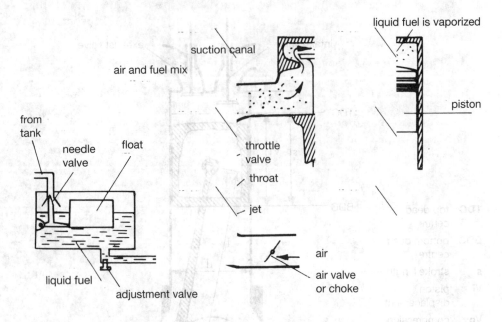

There is no one positive solution. However, internally incoherent things also have an origin somewhere and observe certain principles, even if they are conflictual. Their internal conflicts also have their own origination, their own logic.

The examples given above certainly do not present the only correct method for teaching the functioning of the internal combustion engine. The development of an orientation basis is a task which can always be improved. Furthermore, for the same subject there are almost always several useful points of view, so that "the one and only correct solution" seldom exists.

Five types of orientation bases

Above it has already been indicated that an orientation basis founded on general principles may enable students to develop their own, new orientation bases suitable for individual cases and situations. This is the idea we will further elaborate here by distinguishing between five types of orientation bases.

The first type of an orientation basis is simply an *exemplar*, a *prototype* representing a class or category of objects or phenomena.[5] Such an orientation basis is commonly represented in the form of a picture or mental image. It may also take the form of a metaphor or a story that highlights some presumably crucial features of the phenomenon. This type of an orientation basis does not contain any explicit specification of what are the important features or what is the essential structure of the phenomenon. In this sense, a prototype is holistic and undifferentiated.

The teacher demonstrates how the internal-combustion engine is used or how to regulate its usual functions. The teacher's actions function as a holistic prototype and example.

The decisive junctures which govern the actions are not, however, pointed out, nor is the student give any specific guidance or model for them.

This may be compared to a common way to teach first grade pupils to print letters. The teacher draws an A on the blackboard and asks the children to copy it in their workbooks. According to a study, this method required on average 174 repetitions before the letter is faultlessly learned. Transfer effect to the next letter was poor: on average 163 repetitions were needed before the letter was printed perfectly.[6]

The second type of an orientation basis is a *list* or a *classification* that divides the object or phenomenon in parts and organizes those parts in a hierarchical order. This type of an orientation basis, commonly called an *advance organizer*, is often effective in helping students to organize and recall large amount of textual information.[7]

The student is given a list of the vital parts of the motor, perhaps also a diagram where the parts are located (such as the one presented above in diagram 11). This orientation basis can help the student keep the overall structure of the motor in mind when the teacher goes into the details of its various parts. The details can be *located* in relation to the whole and to each other. However, a static orientation basis such as this will not help the student monitor his or her practical actions on the motor.

The third type of an orientation basis consists of precise instructions for the performance of a task or procedure. Such procedural *algorithms* and rules single out the important successive steps of a performance.[8] They are commonly found in the user's manuals of all kinds of technical devices and appliances. They are often represented in form of flow charts or checklists. They are very helpful in the learning and execution of demanding practical actions. Their limitation is that they offer ready-made "recipes" for a certain procedure without indicating why the procedure must be exactly as presented. When the conditions of the task change, such an orientation basis does not help the student to find out an appropriate alternative procedure.

The student is given, for example, exact stepwise instructions for the adjustment of the ignition of the motor. A different model of the motor may, however, require a quite different procedure which cannot be directly inferred from the algorithm given.

This may be compared to the second variation of the study mentioned above in which first grade pupils were taught to print letters. In this variation, they were given dotted outlines of the letter. This way the proper way of printing the letter was acquired much more quickly than with the method first described. Only 22 repetitions were necessary for the first letter and 17 for the second. Each letter, however, had to be learned by using a separate model – transfer effect from one letter to another was comparatively weak.

The fourth type of an orientation basis describes the object as a system, exposing its internal relations and dynamics. A *systems model* like this enables the student to *diagnose* various states and problems of the system as well as to select and construct appropriate procedures for them.[9] By means of a systems model, the general principle and method are taught which enable the student to create his or her own precise "recipes" for performing many kinds of tasks.

We can again refer to our example from the study which described the teaching of printing letters. In its third variation, the systemic principle of writing the letters was disclosed. They were taught that they could themselves make a model for any letter by placing dots at every point where the line forming a letter should change direction. In other words, the students learned to diagnose letters as systems before reproducing them. In this way the correct writing of the first letter required 14 attempts and the second 8. After the seventh letter, students were able to write any letter correctly after one try. The scope of transfer effect is visible in that the same students were able to learn Arabic and Georgian letters without difficulty and could constructively adapt the principle they had learned to the drawing of various objects.

Systems models are very powerful tools for diagnosing complex interactions. They help the student to realize that there may be many possible causes behind a problem and many alternative routes to a solution. Systems models facilitate probabilistic thinking and coping with uncertainty. However, they often tend to become very complex themselves.

The fifth type of an orientation basis is a model of the basic initial relationships that give rise to more complicated versions of the system. Such a "germ cell" model goes back to the origin of the phenomenon.[10] In the same way that each cell of a living organism contains all the genetic information necessary for the development and activity of that organism, it contains in compact form the necessary elements for the functioning and evolution of the system. The necessary elements and inner relations are manifested in the "germ cell" model in pure form: they have been pruned of all unessential particularities and external variations.

An initiation course is organized for new employees in a large oil refinery to explain to them amongst other things the structure and functioning of the refinery. This is a difficult task. An oil refinery is a very complex system with innumerable technical details. Often students have not been able to satisfactorily understand and appropriate this part of the initiation course.

However, now a lecturer has been found who manages to get the message across and who has himself considered more thoroughly than others the structure and active principle of an oil refinery. He begins his teaching by drawing a simple diagram depicting the functioning of a bootleg distillery. He explains the principle of distillation by this simple example.

The gigantic oil refinery also originates from the principle of distillation, so now the essential components and functions of an oil refinery can be constructed step by step as further diversifications of the simple model of a home distillery.

This lecturer had discovered the "germ cell" common to the home distillery and the oil refinery, namely distillation. The discovery of this sort of simple, basic principle makes it possible to understand a seemingly overpowering and complicated system.

The "germ cell" cannot be understood by mechanically chopping up the parts of the system. The oil refinery and the home distillery are not made up of the same external parts. Similarly, in explaining why water puts out fire, one would be driven astray by separating water into its chemical components, hydrogen and oxygen, for hydrogen burns and oxygen keeps fire going. The particularities of water are explained by studying water molecules and their behaviour as the "germ cell" of water, the tiniest basic unit in which the necessary elements and inner relations of water exist.

Often the "germ cell" can be discovered by means of historical and "genetic" analysis; that is, by tracing the way in which the functional principle of the system in question was originally formed or invented and developed.

The simple dynamic model of the internal-combustion engine depicted in diagram 12 is not sufficiently complex to depict the details of any real modern motor. In its simplicity, it is probably much closer to the ideas and actual prototypes developed by the inventors of the first internal-combustion engines. In that sense, it is more like a "germ cell" model than an accurate systems model.

The "germ cell" model enables the student to reduce complicated phenomena to their root relations and then to reconstruct increasingly complex systems from that root. A "germ cell" model seeks out and explains inner tensions and contradictions at the core of systems, keeping the systems in creative disequilibrium. Thus, a "germ cell" orientation basis helps one to study and understand the *evolution* and qualitative change of a system rather than just diagnose its inner states and problems.

A "germ cell" model is deceptively simple. After it has been discovered and formulated, it looks as if it were self-evident. The limitation of a "germ

Table 1. Five types of orientation bases

Type	Question answered	Typical use	Limitation
1. Prototype	"What is it like?"	Identification, categorization	No inner distinctions
2. Advance organizer	"Where is it located?"	Classification, hierarchization	Static; no dynamics
3. Algorithm	"How to proceed?"	Procedure monitoring	Specific; narrow
4. Systems model	"Why is it like this?" "Why this procedure?"	Diagnosis, selection and construction of procedures	Often very complex
5. "Germ cell" model	"Where does it come from?" "Where is it going to?"	Evolutionary explanation, generation of models of types 1 to 4	Abstract if used alone

cell" model is its very abstractness. It needs to be used as a tool for understanding and constructing systems models, algorithms, advance organizers and prototypes. If a "germ cell" model is only given to students as such, it loses its developmental potential and becomes a platitude.

The five types of orientation basis described above can now be summarized with the help of table 1.

The five types of orientation bases could be depicted as if forming a pyramid (See Annex 1, picture 1). Innumerable specific prototypes make up the broad basis of everyday cognition, upon which more elaborate representations are built. On the top, relatively few systems models and particularly "germ cell" models enable one to have a broad view and explain a wide variety of phenomena. But if cut off from the base layers, the top remains hopelessly abstract and impractical. Thus, the crucial task of good instruction is to facilitate and stimulate the formation and active use of the different types of orientation bases and their combinations, and flexible movement between them.

Orientation, in the form of orientation bases, is fundamentally important for high quality learning. Annex 1, pictures 1-19, give some examples of the above-mentioned five types of orientation basis.

In practice, it seems that students learn relatively easily to produce and use advance organizers and algorithms. But it is commonly very difficult for students and practitioners to construct and apply systems models and "germ cell' models, even in domains in which they have lots of practical experience or book knowledge.[11]

Example 2: Orientation bases for factory inspectors

What might be a "germ cell" model for understanding the work of factory inspectors?

From the very beginnings of factory inspection, at least the following four components must have been brought together: a *factory*, an *inspector*, a *set of norms and tools*, and a somehow standardized *inspection procedure*. Thus, we get the tentative model depicted in diagram 14.

In diagram 14, each connecting arrow represents interaction, tension, and potential conflict. On the basis of the "germ cell", we can now construct systems models for each of the four historical types of inspectors' work presented in diagram 10 in Chapter 2. As examples, we shall here present systems models for the traditional enforcement type of factory inspector's work (diagram 15) and for the emerging new advisory and consultative type of factory inspector's work (diagram 16).

Diagram 15 represents the traditional enforcement or "police" model of factory inspector's work. The basic purpose of inspection work according to that model is to control that the working conditions comply with the provisions of the law. The inspector needs thorough knowledge of the individual chapters and clauses of the law and means to apply them to individual work environments.

Diagram 14: A "germ cell" model of factory inspection work

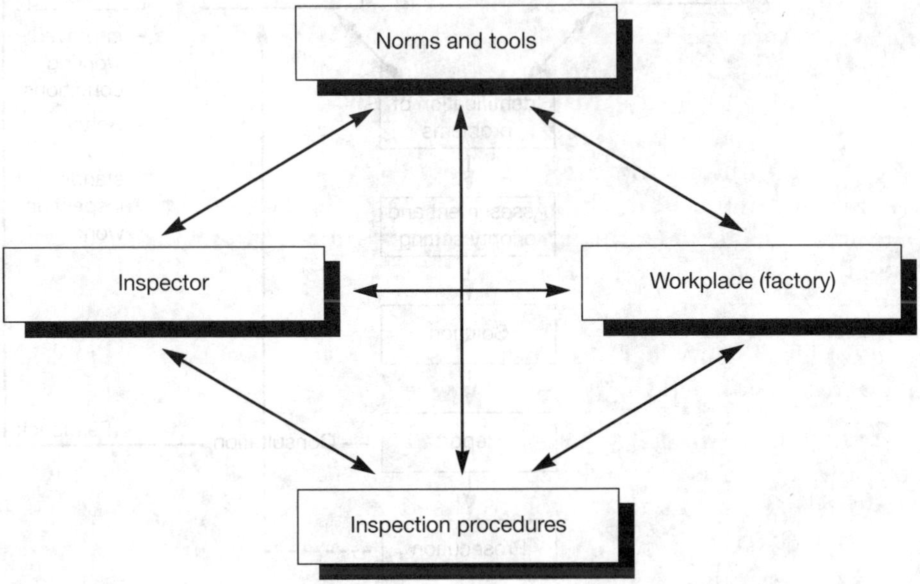

Diagram 15: A systems model of the traditional enforcement type of factory inspection work

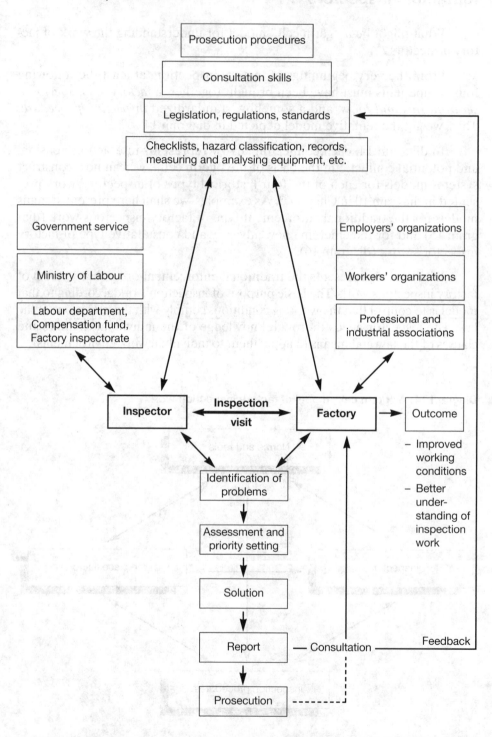

Diagram 16: A systems model of the emerging advisory and consultative type of factory inspection work

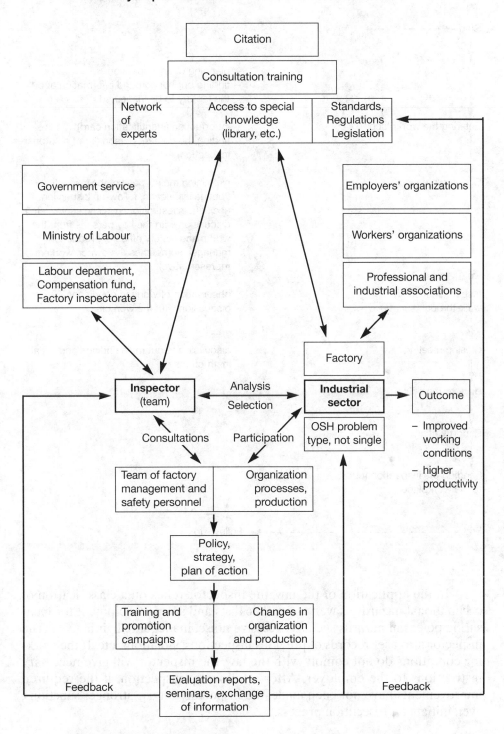

**Diagram 17: A algorithm for the standard inspection procedure typical of
the enforcement model of factory inspection work**

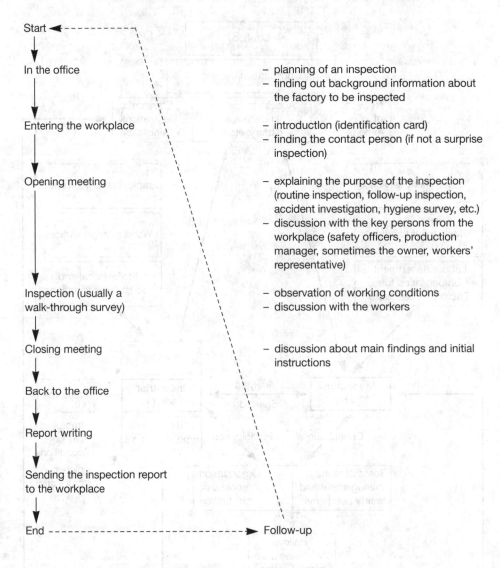

Start

In the office
- planning of an inspection
- finding out background information about the factory to be inspected

Entering the workplace
- introductlon (identification card)
- finding the contact person (if not a surprise inspection)

Opening meeting
- explaining the purpose of the inspection (routine inspection, follow-up inspection, accident investigation, hygiene survey, etc.)
- discussion with the key persons from the workplace (safety officers, production manager, sometimes the owner, workers' representative)

Inspection (usually a walk-through survey)
- observation of working conditions
- discussion with the workers

Closing meeting
- discussion about main findings and initial instructions

Back to the office

Report writing

Sending the inspection report to the workplace

End — — — — — — — — — — — — — — — — — — ▶ Follow-up

In the application of the law, the inspector relies on a classification of occupational hazards as well as on checklists and special equipment for measuring potential hazards such as excessive noise, inadequate lighting, etc. The inspector also uses records of previous inspections, violations, etc. If the working conditions do not comply with the law, the inspector will give necessary instructions to the employer. After a follow-up inspection, if the required improvements have not been made, the inspector will use stronger sanctions, even initiate a prosecution process.

Diagram 16 depicts the emerging advisory and consultative type of factory inspectors' work. Although it can still be constructed around the same "germ cell", as a system it is very different from the traditional enforcement model. The work is no longer performed by an individual inspector but by a team of inspectors consulting workplaces and enterprises in the design and implementation of production systems and processes. The object of inspectors' work is dramatically broader and more complex than the discrete hazards in one factory. Now the inspectors deal with entire industrial sectors and branches. The inspectors' tools include networks of experts and modern information services. The inspectors also rely on training and consultation techniques as important tools.

On the basis of systems models like these, we can identify relevant algorithms and advance organizers. The traditional enforcement model is heavily dependent on an algorithm that singles out the steps of a standard inspection procedure. Such an algorithm is presented in diagram 17.

The traditional enforcement model also uses classifications of hazards which can be represented and taught with the help of advance organizers like the one depicted in diagram 18.

Numerous similar examples of more specific orientation bases could be derived from the same root. The crucial point is that the various models interact and that the students move between them, up and down in the pyramid of orientation. That way, the students can also learn to invent and construct novel models on their own.

Drawing up an orientation basis

One might begin to formulate an orientation basis by asking what kind of performance one is after. At this stage, the desired performance might be described as external "behaviour". However, not just one particular performance needs to be described. The question is rather what types of performance, varying in changing circumstances, should the student be capable of. Thus it appears that all the possible types of performance can hardly be foreseen, let alone meaningfully described as discrete behaviours apart from each other.

This is only the beginning, however. Next one needs to ask: Why is one procedure correct and another wrong? What are the principles? How did the phenomenon originate?

The source and principle must now be linked to practice, that is to say, put into a concrete form of action or fulfillment. The most universally applicable and yet simplest form must be chosen so that the orientation basis is neither too limiting nor too complicated.

Diagram 18: An advance organizer for the classification of hazards[12]

Hazard type	Sources	Effects
1. Mechanical	machines, transport ways, floors, ladders, disorder	wounds, cuts, bruises, fractures, death
2. Physical		
a) Noise and vibration	vibrating objects; flow of air, liquid or gas	temporary or permanent hearing loss, vibration disease, psychosocial harm and disability
b) Electricity	electric current, electric arc	burns, electric shock, death
c) Radiation	sun, some lasers, microwave ovens, RF heaters, atomic detonation, X-rays, radioactive materials	glare and eye irritation, skin and other tissue injuries, genetic disorders
d) Climatic conditions (the balance between people and environment is important)	temperature, humidity, radiation, air velocity, air cleanliness (combination)	heat cramps, exhaustion and stroke (dehydration), cold, freezing (frostbite)
e) Illumination and color design (correct lighting conditions are important)	natural lighting, artificial lighting	fatigue, accidents (indirectly)
3. Chemical hazards	chemicals, toxic materials and wastes, fires and explosions	irritation and inflammation, allergies, burns, acute and chronic poisoning, genetic disorders, cancer
4. Biological hazards (these hazards are present in health care, in agriculture and in the food processing industry)	bacteria, virus, fungus	occupational diseases
5. Physiological hazards	heavy workload; monotonous, repetitive work; unsuitable tools and controls; wrong working methods	fatigue, strain injuries, back diseases
6. Psychosocial hazards	quality of work (monotonous, continuous alertness, working alone, etc.), human relations	discomfort, irritation, psychosomatic diseases, mental diseases

After this, the points of view thus formulated need to be turned into an initial model, an orientation basis. It should be lucid and clear. It should serve as an aid to thought or as a map guiding real task performances. It must also be a help in controlling and evaluating outcomes. This kind of model also reveals the instructor's own basic assumptions which can lead to critical discussion.

Finally, the usefulness of an orientation basis must be checked by discussing it, for instance, with colleagues and experts in the field. It should be evaluated both from the point of view of contents as well as of pedagogical form. Specially important is to judge whether tasks related to the subject may truly be supported by this orientation basis.

Often an introductory, even inadequate orientation basis will help students to a surprising degree. It gives them a point of interest, a framework in which they can consciously and systematically espouse new actions and concepts. At its best it is also an aid one can rely on over and over again in performing different tasks and evaluating one's own work.

The initial orientation basis should be used as a springboard for the construction of complementary and more specific variations. Nevertheless, the orientation bases for separate aspects of the subject matter should be tied up with the general orientation basis of the entire domain or course.

Difficulties of forming an orientation basis

Often in the beginning, drawing up an orientation basis is difficult and one makes mistakes. Experience has revealed the following typical pitfalls:

1. Patterns of thought and action to be learnt and instructional means of attaining them often get confused in the orientation basis. "Lecture" or "drills" even get noted in orientation bases. But these things do not belong to the pattern to be learned: they are only methods for teaching the model.

2. The orientation basis is left far too much on the level of haphazard generalities and nomenclature. "The general principles of factory inspector's work" are stated for instance, but what those principles are is not told. This is a common weakness which appears in the first stages of outlining a basis. It is linked to the fact that the principles are not traced to their source nor are they sufficiently related to practice. They are just loosely asserted.

3. The orientation basis simply states the subject matter and topics successively, like a list of contents. The inter-relations between them are not noticed. They are not fashioned into an active whole which could come to the assistance of thought. In other words, the orientation basis is left at the level of an advance organizer without considering the possible advantages of more dynamic models.

4. Another common mistake is to formulate an orientation basis which is too complex, which includes too much material and too many individual points. In this case the core gets easily lost in the complicated presentation.

5. Finally, there are the risks of using too many terms which are unfamiliar to students and reducing the orientation basis to a minimum abstraction. One attempts to present everything in one outline or in a few abstract terms with insufficient explanations. In this case the subject becomes incomprehensible or deceptively simple. No association is made between the orientation basis and students' world of everyday thought and experience.

There is no one correct and definitive model for an orientation basis. Fixed directions cannot be drawn up which would suit all learning contents and contexts.

The instructional use of orientation bases

Imagine an explorer. He thought he had charted the unknown parts of a region, but now he has heard a rumour that in the middle of it there is an area still unexplored. Faced with this conflict, he decides to set out and find this undiscovered area. In a sense, this is his "behavioural objective". But the real work begins only after this.

What must he do to make the voyage succeed? He must analyse the map of the region and study why this area was left undiscovered. He must formulate a concise hypothesis or theory which will guide and stimulate him in finding the area he is seeking. This becomes his *"germ cell"* model. He subsequently enriches and elaborates it into *systems models* which take into account the interaction of all kinds of factors: weather conditions, equipment, availability of food and water, etc.

Based on the above, he will trace the possible routes to take and alternative ways of advancing. He must draw up a stepwise plan for his trip. This plan is an *algorithmic* orientation basis of his voyage. He also makes lists of items he has to carry with him – they are examples of *advance organizer* orientation bases needed for the endeavour.

At the beginning of his trip, he has to continually use his theory and plan and lists in problematic situations – in recognizing landmarks, selecting alternative routes and choosing campsites, for instance. Gradually, he *internalizes* his orientation bases. He no longer needs to read them or work with pencil and paper so often. The models begin to "live" in his thoughts.

In using the orientation bases, he ends up testing them as well. Their lacunae show up. During the trip they can be partially corrected and made more accurate. With the help of the orientation bases, the explorer can evaluate his progress:

"Have I stuck to my plan or even surpassed it? Have I solved problems on the basis of my theory or rather instinctively and erroneously?"

At its best, studying can be compared to the work of an explorer. The student conquers an unknown territory of knowledge and skills. Sadly enough, far too often the student's toil resembles more the alienated work of the explorer's paid bearer. Like the bearer, the student feels it makes no difference what territory he or she is covering.

The instructor should turn students into explorers. An orientation basis is a great tool for attaining this. But it must be used with care and consideration. The instructional uses of an orientation basis can be divided into its formation, its internalization, and its use in controlling performance.

Forming an orientation basis

An orientation basis should not be simply shown or given ready-made to students in the beginning of the course. Discovering and shaping it is an instructional task in itself, which is very important for the continuation of instruction. The explorer does not get his travel plans "ready-packaged"; he has to shape them himself by solving a series of problems. This is also the case in instruction. Students should design the orientation basis for themselves as a solution to the motivating cognitive conflict aroused at the beginning of instruction. In other words, the starting point is a problem, a conflict. An orientation basis is needed to solve it.

For example, in teaching the use of the internal-combustion engine, one could start out from the problematic situation that the motor doesn't work. What can be done? In searching for different answers, it is soon noticed that the fault might be due to any number of reasons. How can we go about sensibly checking the most probable reason? The students will have difficulty in arguing for one given solution over another, for they do not clearly comprehend the overall idea of the motor. At that point it is decided that the functional idea of the motor must be mastered as a whole. They begin to analyse it. An orientation basis, or several competing sketches for it, are arrived at by utilizing students' own experience and experiments with the motor. Finally, the orientation basis is formulated as a diagram.

The orientation basis, then, should be an insight to students and not something simply given from above. Nor does the formation of an orientation basis need to be limited to the early stages of instruction. It can be completed, revised and developed in later stages of the learning cycle.

The internalization of orientation bases

Earlier on we stated that internalization and externalization are closely related in the integral learning process. Similarly, thorough internalization of an orientation basis is conditioned by its use as a help in performing various tasks.

In 1908 C. H. Judd reported an experiment which was to become famous. He compared the results of two groups of students who had been given the task of aiming darts at objects placed under water. Hitting the mark proved difficult, because the direction of light is curved in water differently than in air and results in an optical illusion for the person observing the object and the dart.

Prior to the exercise, one group had been taught the theory of the refraction of light. The other group had to aim at the object on the basis of trial and error.

In the first phase of the experiment, when the object was placed at a constant depth, one group learned to hit the mark as quickly as the other. But in the second phase, the depth of the object was changed. In this case the group which had received theoretical teaching learned very quickly to hit the object at new depths, while the other group continued to advance by trial and error. The students in the latter group tried first to use the "fixed" method they had just acquired. This rendered it difficult to switch to a new, adapted method and so their achievement of a precise aim was slow.[13]

The results of Judd's experiment, and many other studies inspired by it, indicate that an orientation which explains the theoretical foundations of the performance or material to be learned can be a real benefit to instruction, especially when it must be applied to new tasks. At the moment of novel application, the orientation basis begins to "live" and its potential is revealed.

What kinds of tasks could be performed with the help of the orientation basis of the internal-combustion engine?

By adapting Judd's example, we can think of an experimental situation in which two groups of students are made to study a motor which for some reason will not start. The students are asked to search for the fault and correct it. Prior to this, one group has formulated the orientation basis (the motor's functional principle in a simplified model), the other not. It may be that in the first task both groups perform equally. In the second, some functional defect has been situated in the motor. Most likely, the group which has drawn up an orientation basis will already cope more quickly and correctly than the group which works under trial and error.

An orientation basis can also be used as a help in exercising given performances so that they become automatic and shortened routines. It is most important, however, that these specific performances are connected to broader, overall orientation bases so that when solving an isolated problem, the individual is able to choose an appropriate performance and when necessary, solve the problem by conscious deliberation.

Performance control with the help of an orientation basis

When a student performs a task, he or she can use an orientation basis to help control and revise his or her progress. Control does not come into play only with the final outcome. It should be present in each stage. With the help of an orientation basis, control can develop into the students' own control and self-monitoring.

In the first tasks, students can lean directly on the orientation basis. Later on, they may be given tasks for which they no longer have at hand a visible orientation basis, but must resort to the model they have internalized. The visible model may be used as an aid to evaluation once the task has been completed, or if performance is not yet mastered on the internalized model.

Students must look for the fault without having the diagram of the motor in front of them. At different stages, they are asked to describe how they are proceeding and to give reasons why they are doing what they are doing. After this the orientation basis is brought out and used to evaluate whether or not the method used by the students was the best. Did they apply the functional principles of the motor, or did they proceed by trial and error?

Orientation bases as facilitators of collaborative learning

Jay McTighe has recently analysed the benefits of orientation bases, or "graphic organizers" as he calls them, for collaborative learning.[14] He lists them as follows:

1. They provide a focal point for group discussions by offering a common frame of reference for thinking.

2. The completed graphic orientation basis provides a "group memory" or tangible product of the group's discussion.

3. By working with a graphic orientation basis as part of a collaborative group, students are encouraged to expand their own thinking by considering different points of view.

4. The articulation of reasoning required by the use of a graphic orientation basis helps to render the invisible process of thinking visible for all participants.

The most persistent obstacle to successful collaboration is the difficulty of formulating a shared representation of the object to be mastered. Effective collaboration requires that the point of view of the other members of a group can be realistically imagined. Drafting and modifying different versions of a graphic orientation basis enables students to see each other's ideas and thus take each other's perspectives. Recently computer programs have been developed to support such collaborative construction of orientation bases.[15]

---

[1] The idea of behavioural objectives was popular, even dominant, in the instructional planning of the 1960s and 1970s. It represents an attempt to make instruction strictly controlled and rationalized much in the same fashion as time-motion studies and assembly lines were used to rationalize industrial work. For handbooks on behavioural objectives, see Armstrong et al. (1970); Kibler, Barker & Miles (1970); McAshan (1970); Mager (1962); Vargas (1972). The growing criticism against the exclusive use of behavioural objectives was reflected in Kapfer (1978).

[2] See Gallwey (1974) for an analysis of "the inner game of tennis".

[3] The concept of orientation basis was originally developed by P. J. Gal'perin (1969; 1989; 1992). He pointed out the significance of orientation in all human actions and formulated a theory of the stepwise formation of skills and concepts (see also Talyzina, 1981).

[4] Bransford and Johnson (1972) showed experimentally that even short texts are much better understood and recalled when they begin with headings than when they have no headings or when a heading is given only at the end of the text. Research on so-called advance organizers gives additional support to this finding (see Ausubel, 1963; Ausubel, Novak & Hanesian, 1978; Mayer, 1979).

[5] Prototypes have been extensively studied by Rosch and her associates (see Rosch & Lloyd, 1978).

[6] This example is taken from a well-known study made by N. S. Pantina, extensively presented in Talyzina (1981, p. 92-94) and in Gal'perin (1992).

[7] See Ausubel (1963); Ausubel, Novak & Hanesian (1978); Mayer (1979).

[8] The instructional uses of algorithms and rules have been studied by Landa (1974) and Scandura (1976).

[9] Among the large literature on systems models, the "soft systems methodology" of Checkland and his associates (Checkland, 1981; Checkland & Scholes, 1990) may be mentioned as an example of instructionally promising applications.

[10] See Davydov (1988; 1990).

[11] Axelrod and his colleagues give interesting evidence of this in their studies of the cognitive maps of policy makers (Axelrod, 1976).

[12] See Vähäpassi (1991).

[13] See Judd (1908).

[14] See McTighe (1992).

[15] See Boland et al. (1992).

SELECTION AND ORGANIZATION OF INSTRUCTIONAL CONTENTS

5

From static packages to toolkits for mastering continuous change

Teachers commonly rely on textbooks and pre-packaged instructional materials in the selection of instructional contents. In work-related training of adults, standard curricula, textbooks and teaching packages often do not exist. The need for training increasingly often stems from changes in work practices.

The selection of instructional contents in work-related training is based on analyses of competences and skills required in practice. But practice can no longer be understood as a collection of static individual job descriptions and standardized lists of discrete skills. Robert Reich argues that the global markets are increasingly dependent on what he calls "symbolic-analytic services".

"Symbolic analysts solve, identify, and broke problems by manipulating symbols. They simplify reality into abstract images that can be rearranged, juggled, experimented with, communicated to other specialists, and then, eventually, transformed back into reality. The manipulations are done with analytic tools, sharpened by experience. The tools may be mathematical algorithms, legal arguments, financial gimmicks, scientific principles, psychological insights about how to persuade or to amuse, systems of induction or deduction, or any other set of techniques for doing conceptual puzzles.

"(...) Symbolic analysts often work alone or in small teams, which may be connected to larger organizations, including worldwide webs. Teamwork is often critical.

"Since neither problems nor solutions can be defined in advance, frequent and informal conversations help ensure that insights and discoveries are put to their best uses and subjected to quick, critical evaluation."[1]

Larry Hirschhorn and Shoshana Zuboff[2] demonstrate that this vision applies to industrial and clerical work as well as to traditional professions. "Intellective skills' and "developmental work", that is, involvement in contin-

Diagram 19: Investigative learning and work practice

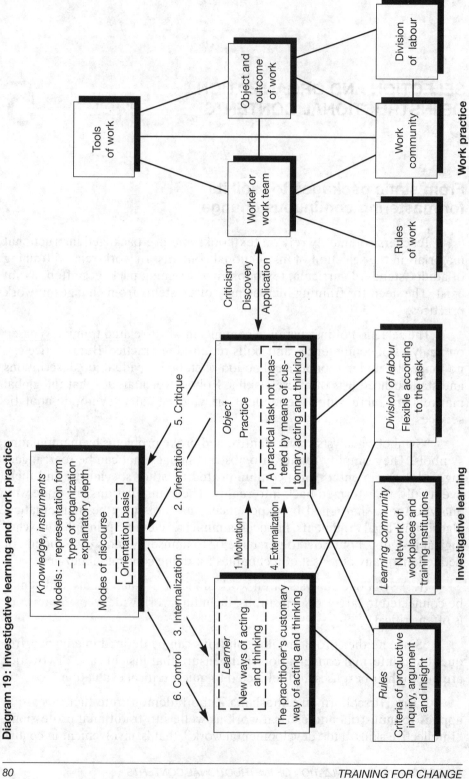

Work practice

- Tools of work
- Object and outcome of work
- Division of labour
- Worker or work team
- Work community
- Rules of work

Criticism
Discovery
Application

Investigative learning

Knowledge, instruments
Models: – representation form
– type of organization
– explanatory depth
Modes of discourse
[Orientation basis]

5. Critique
2. Orientation
3. Internalization
6. Control

Object
Practice
[A practical task not mastered by means of customary acting and thinking]

1. Motivation
4. Externalization

Learner
[New ways of acting and thinking]
The practitioner's customary way of acting and thinking

Division of labour
Flexible according to the task

Learning community
Network of workplaces and training institutions

Rules
Criteria of productive inquiry, argument and insight

uous redesign of the ongoing work practice, are central to the evolving new forms of work organization.

"Because sociotechnical settings encourage member learning and development, the number and range of rules, procedures, and authority relations governing behaviour are smaller than in conventional settings. The resulting uncertainty can create tension and anxiety, but it is this very tension that provides the space and the sanction for creative and innovative behaviour."[3]

We live in the midst of a pervasive transition from rigid mass production to flexible and customized production, from hierarchical organizations to teams and network-like organizational patterns. Teams and networks call for a multiskilled collaborative workforce instead of narrow specialization.

"The new requirement for the typical worker, then, is three major steps beyond yesterday's 'pair of hands': She or he should (a) be multiskilled; (b) choose and master an area of special competence; and (c) transmit that special knowledge to others, within and beyond the work team's borders."[4]

All this implies that instructional contents must be seen as flexible and changing toolkits for mastering a comprehensive practice rather than as fixed bodies of compartmentalized knowledge to be memorized. The selection of the intellectual tools to be taught should be based on careful analyses of change in the work practice.

In many cases, the instructional process itself can contain such an analysis of the changing work practice. Instead of merely telling the students what they should learn, it is often much more productive to let the students visit workplaces, interview practitioners, collect historical documents, read literature, and synthesize their findings with the help of models of the work activity. Such inquiry provides a rich basis for motivation. orientation and practical application tasks in the learning cycle.

The need to analyse the changing work practice as an integral part of instruction calls for an extension of the basic model of investigative learning presented earlier in diagram 8. In diagram 19, the investigative learning cycle is connected to work practice.

Notice that investigative learning is not subordinated to the work practice in a one-way fashion. The connection is more complex than that. First of all, investigative learning analyses and criticizes the work practice in an historical perspective – learners identify problems and contradictions in the work practice (the context of criticism). Secondly, investigative learning discovers and appropriates intellectual tools and models – orientation bases – for mastering and developing the work practice (the context of discovery). Thirdly, investigative learning applies and practises the newly formulated intellectual tools in actual tasks of the work practice (the context of application).

Which is more important, content or form?

The objectives for a certain course on creativity were specified in the following way:

o   Consciousness of the importance of creative activity both at work and in private life;

o   self-confidence to use one's creative ability;

o   sensitivity to problems and possibilities in one's surroundings, an attitude of "constructive discontent" towards one's environment;

o   courage to accept and develop ideas with an open mind;

o   skill to produce new and good ideas, to fulfil them while heeding the actual limits set by practice.

This example starts with the idea that creativity can be trained and developed independently of the contents and contexts in which it shall be applied. The same course, then, could suit members of any occupation or organization. Creativity is seen as a formal characteristic in which specific practices and associated specific knowledge are of little importance.

"The prerequisite for productive creativity is a sensitive and broad ability to perceive things from several viewpoints and a courageous, independent and self-confident attitude. Yet this is not enough: one also needs the skill to throw oneself into the world of imagination and play as well as a strong, innovative will."

This is how it is stated by those who market the course. They say nothing of a possible need for meaningful knowledge and mastery of one's work, the thing one hopes to influence through this creative attitude.

But could Albert Einstein, for example – undeniably a creative person – have succeeded in developing the theory of relativity just by observing things sensitively, broadly, and from several points of view? Were courage, originality and a self-confident attitude, imagination and an innovative will, enough for Einstein? He certainly did have these characteristics. But his achievements were founded on years of solid, systematic work to acquire a deep substantive mastery of physics. Without that, he would not have become a creative scientist.

It may even be stated that no one becomes a really creative leader, planner or employee unless one has a good substantive mastery of one's own field of work. Ideas and imagination require nourishment. They do not develop apart from meaningful and useful contents.

The example of a course on creativity is not unique. Comparable traits are found abundantly in programmes of courses on critical thinking, interaction, communication and different leadership skills. Form is emphasized to the detriment of content.[5]

Peculiar to this way of thinking is to hold methods and atmosphere as the decisive criteria of a course. To learn to be creative, you have to be inspired and in a liberated mood; to learn interactive skills, you need to be trained in sensitivity and insight. But this line of thought disregards concepts and substantive ideas as tools of thought and action.

Where has such an emphasis come from? Why has it gained so much popularity?

The spreading of this way of thinking is at least partly an expression of discontent with both the traditional way of grinding facts into memory and the more recent demand to train fixed, isolated performances. It has been quite accurately felt that by mechanically pressing isolated facts into the student's head, one inhibits creative thought and independent and critical development. But from this, it has been too lightly inferred that knowledge is generally a hindrance to the development of human personality.

Thus the overemphasis on form is largely due to not being able to distinguish between qualitatively different types of knowledge. All knowledge is looked upon in the same way as memorabilia or heavy "book learning". This stems from a misconceived and unfruitful opposition between form and content.

In the absence of content, instruction loses the significance it has had for ages as the transmission of evolved knowledge and skills, of culture and civilization, from one generation to the next. When form and formal characteristics, divorced from content, become pre-eminent in instruction, we drift into a situation in which we no longer strive to teach something new to students, but entertain them.

However, it is not the amount of knowledge which is important, but its content and quality. A kind of knowledge is needed which is the basis and tool of critical thought and creative activity, not their obstruction.

What kind of knowledge fulfils these requirements?

Empirical knowledge and theoretical knowledge

There is a type of knowledge that differs markedly from fixed, dished-out facts and schematic performances, as well as from mere formal abilities. Following V. V. Davydov, it may be called *theoretical knowledge*. It can also be characterized as theoretical concepts, or as a theoretical relationship to reality.[6]

These terms immediately rouse opposition in many minds. Isn't theory dry, irrelevant to life and difficult to learn? How can it now serve creative thought?

This way of thinking can most certainly be traced back to bad experiences of learning "theory" in courses and educational institutions. Often courses in fact do include a segment for theory, served as a set of fixed definitions and disconnected from practical applications and skills taught afterwards. Such contents should not be called theoretical – scholastic is a better term for them.

Indeed, theory is commonly spoiled or taught poorly. An essential feature of genuine theory is that it helps to master practical things and activities. If this is not established in instruction, theory is being done an injustice. If it cannot be established, the theory being taught is probably spurious, unfounded wordmongering.

But what is ultimately meant by genuine theoretical knowledge? Karmiloff-Smith and Inhelder provide a nice illustration of what is at stake.

The researchers presented children with a relatively difficult block balancing task. The children typically sought immediate solution; they were happy when the blocks balanced and unhappy when they did not balance. The researchers called this approach the "action response" or "success orientation"; one could also call it the empirical approach. However, a different approach emerged in the midst of the dominant one.

"Frequently, even when children were successful in balancing an item on one dimension (...) , they went on exploring the other dimensions of each block. It was as if their attention were momentarily diverted from their goal of balancing to what had started as a subgoal, i.e., the search for means. One could see the children oscillating between seeking the goal and seeking to "question" the block."

The authors call the latter "theory response". Within that approach, the child does not measure his or her success with the immediate outcome (balanced or not balanced), but rather with verification or falsification of his or her theory. If the child's theory predicts that the block will not balance, he or she will rejoice when it indeed doesn't. "At this point we witness experimentation for the experimentation's sake; for attending to the means implies seeking knowledge of the approximate range of possible actions on an object."[7]

This experiment demonstrates that theory should not be regarded as something immutable and fixed. Theoretical knowledge has the character of continuous questioning and self-revision. The crucial difference is that empirical knowledge asks "what?" and "how?", while theoretical knowledge asks "why?". Empirical knowledge is satisfied with getting a correct answer or successful solution. Theoretical knowledge asks why the answer was correct, why the solution was successful. In that sense, theoretical knowledge is insatiable. It implies risk taking and uncertainty. It incessantly endeavours to step into unknown territory.

Empirical knowledge takes the form of specific end solutions, answers and definitions. Theoretical knowledge manifests itself in general means for reaching and formulating variable specific end solutions, answers and definitions. The core of theoretical knowledge is to be found in such powerful intellectual procedures as historical analysis, experimentation, detection of contradictions, and modelling. However, these are not formal and abstract procedures void of contents. They can be mastered and creatively applied only in unity with substantive contents of some specific field of research or practice. In this sense, theoretical knowledge transcends the dichotomy and opposition between form and content.

When one knows the names, external appearance and functions of the most commonly used parts of a motor, this is empirical knowledge. Knowledge is theoretical when one understands the functional principles of the motor. Theoretical knowledge is not necessarily verbal. It can be represented in various ways. Often practical physical actions are better indicators of theoretical knowledge than words. We tend to hide our lacking understanding behind empty words.

On the other hand, practical actions alone are often insufficient for grasping and representing theoretical ideas. For thousands of years people have known how to boil water and prepare food, but only a few can explain the laws of molecular physics which are active in the boiling process. More and more benefits, however, are being derived from a mastery of such laws. They permit us to explain many phenomena which are surprising and inconceivable through common sense and experience. To represent and utilize practically such laws and principles, words, diagrams, and mathematical symbols are often necessary.

Between theoretical and empirical knowledge, there is no absolute and everlasting distinction. Our experiences and observations are modified and filtered by the historically evolving concepts and models imposed upon and offered to us by culture. What was new, challenging theoretical knowledge a few hundreds of years ago may now be regarded as everyday empirical knowledge. Contrary to our ancestors, we now "see" the sun as a centre around which our earth rotates. On the other hand, empirical experience often gives rise to new problems and questions which oblige us to develop new theoretical hypotheses and ideas.

How should curricular contents be organized?

A very common problem in work-related adult education is the fragmentation of training into countless separate sessions and courses, difficult to see as an interconnected meaningful whole. Acting like a fire-brigade, we organize a training session every time an important sounding theme or problem arises.

Over time, this situation is unsatisfactory for both trainees and trainers. Trainees cannot systematically develop themselves and their professional skills. Trainers become organizers who do not have time to reflect upon any issue properly.

This is not a new problem. For a long time educational institutions have been saying that there is too much isolated information to be taught. Knowledge should be organized and grouped in some meaningful and justifiable way.

To solve this problem, educators have divided knowledge into subjects of study, more or less according to the division and ordering of scientific disciplines. Clearly defined subjects are seen as a way to ensure systematic, logically continuous formation of concepts. On the other hand, the division of learning into subjects or disciplines has been criticized time and again for the fragmentation it entails. It is pointed out that the solution of complex problems both in natural sciences and in social reality requires increasingly cross-disciplinary or multidisciplinary approaches. Boundaries between scientific disciplines are melting away and new hybrid branches of scientific research emerge at a rapid pace. Integrated topics or projects are seen as the alternative to traditional subjects and disciplines.

Both viewpoints have their merits and weaknesses. In work-related training of adults, courses are often brief and a discipline-based curriculum is out of question. The danger of focusing narrowly on immediately marketable discrete skills is imminent. In these cases, the relevant disciplines may be regarded as healthy sources for constructing systematic conceptual structures and for overcoming superficial teaching in the name of short-sighted "practicality".

In traditional school instruction, the dominant unit of instruction is the lesson. It is a standardized format, typically 45 to 60 minutes in duration. Instruction is planned for one lesson at a time. Students learn to proceed in small, isolated chunks of subject matter. For each lesson, a certain limited amount of textbook contents and homework must be accomplished.

From the viewpoint of the internal factors of instruction, the isolated lesson is not an appropriate unit of planning and execution. It is too short and rigidly bounded for the complex process of investigative learning. The unit of instructional planning must fulfil four requirements.

First, it must be a relatively independent and complete substantive theme. It can be called a *thematic unit*.[8]

Secondly, the kernel of this thematic unit must be some important new theoretical insight or instructionally worthy concept.

Thirdly, the contents of the thematic unit must be organized in such a way that theoretical insight can be linked to practical application.

Fourthly, the duration and scope of the thematic unit must be sufficient to allow for the realization of a complete cycle of investigative learning. Typically a thematic unit covers several successive lessons or other forms of instruction and learning.

It is for each thematic unit that one draws up an orientation basis. Drawing support from the orientation basis, one designs the thematic unit so that students proceed through it stepwise, from motivation and orientation right through to internalization, externalization and critique, and control.

Although each thematic unit is relatively independent, coming one after the other, they must be interconnected and form a broader whole. The theoretical insights contained in the different thematic units form the "plot", the "red thread' of the subject matter. The thematic unit and the insight at its core are like one ring in a chain. The demand for integral learning also holds true for the whole chain. Each thematic unit in it has its own role to play. One might primarily motivate and orientate students within an entire course; another might be predominantly geared to externalization and practical application.

---

[1] Reich, 1992, pp. 178-179.

[2] See Hirschhorn, 1984; Zuboff, 1988.

[3] Hirschhorn, 1984, p. 128.

[4] Peters, 1992, p. 444; see also Cole, 1989; Senge, 1990.

[5] For a critique of such formalism and an alternative view, see McPeck (1990). For a thoughtful assessment of programmes aimed at teaching thinking, see Resnick (1987a).

[6] See Davydov (1990).

[7] See Karmiloff-Smith & Inhelder, 1975, p. 201 and pp. 207-208.

[8] The term thematic unit is used here to emphasize the importance of meaningful thematic contents in the design of such units of instruction. The more commonly used term would be curriculum unit.

METHODS OF INSTRUCTION

6

Classification of teaching methods

What instructional methods are being used in the following example?

Lecturer M. M. introduces a new proposal for legislation on workplace safety and health. He explains the background of the proposal and then goes through it point by point. At the end of his presentation, course participants pose questions and a lively discussion ensues. Then groups of five are formed to consider the effects of the new proposal on the activities of regional factory inspectorates. At the end of the day, representatives of each group present the results of their reflection.

We might answer that in this example, four methods of instruction are used: lecture, discussion, group work, and student presentation.

This is a correct answer, but also very inadequate. It is limited to the *external aspect of instructional methods.* By the external aspect, we mean observable interaction associated with instruction. Attention is focused on who is presenting information and on how participants are grouped.

The external aspect of the teaching method is immediately observable when you step into an instructional situation. You see right away what is taking place: a lecture, a discussion, group or individual work. However, what you do not see is the most essential aspect of instruction: the kind of mental work being accomplished at any given moment. This is called the *internal aspect of instructional methods.*

The same external form of teaching may serve completely different internal purposes, or aim at different steps in the cycle of investigative learning.

M. M.'s lecture may be conveying new knowledge. But it may also contain elements of motivation and orientation towards a new subject. Or it may concentrate entirely on restructuring and systematizing subject matter already learnt.

The internal aspect of instructional methods, the *instructional function* of each moment, cannot be discerned except by following and analysing the longer instructional process. The internal characteristics of an instructional procedure are only explained when one sees the place and importance of a given phase within the *complete instructional treatment* of the subject matter, when one sees why a particular procedure had to be just so at a given stage and the whole process to which it is linked.

The external and internal aspects of a method can be distinguished for *every instructional situation*. The external aspect is seen in the *instructional format* (who is communicating or working) and in the social mode (how participants are grouped). The internal aspect refers to the *instructional function* of each phase of teaching (the kind of mental activity and the step of the learning process which the instructor hopes to achieve). The relations of these concepts are schematized in diagram 20.

The choice of teaching methods is ill-founded if the instructor is only aware of the external aspects. In such a case, the instructor is usually attempting to guarantee variation and external student activeness, driven by the idea that teaching must not be too teacher-centred and monotonous. This typically means that while lectures remain the core of instruction, discussion, group work and exercises are arranged around them as if in order to alleviate and compensate for the overloading and passivizing effects of lectures.

However, mere variation and student activeness do not guarantee good learning. The instructional formats and social modes are only the outer framework for the learning process. Variation and activeness are necessary, of course, but alone they are inadequate preconditions for good learning.

One-sided emphasis on the external aspects of teaching methods easily leads to misconceived conclusions. A person might prefer one certain format or mode, group work for instance, and therefore brand another form, for example the lecture, as bad and unfavourable because it "renders students passive". Such rigid ideas lead to mechanical instruction. The instructor forgets that the value of the format and mode depends upon the function associated with that particular phase of instruction. There is no general distinction between "good" and "bad" teaching formats and modes. To say that lectures "render students passive" indicates that one has not understood the decisive importance of the students' mental, internal activity in learning. A lecture is seen to make the listener passive because he or she displays little external activeness. However, a well-planned lecture may stir up varied and intensive mental activity on the part of the listener.

Instructional formats

Instructional formats can be divided into three main groups: presentations, independent assignments, and cooperative instruction. In a presentation, communication goes one way, from the person making the presentation to those who receive it. Independent assignments are carried out by students with no immedi-

Diagram 20: The external and internal aspects of instructional methods

Methods of instruction

External aspect	Internal aspect
Observable forms of teaching and interaction: who is communicating or working and how?	Guidance of the students' mental work: what kind of learning is being accomplished?

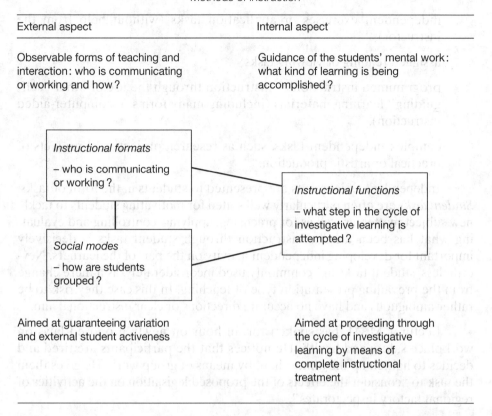

Aimed at guaranteeing variation and external student activeness

Aimed at proceeding through the cycle of investigative learning by means of complete instructional treatment

ate interaction with or help from the instructor. In cooperative instruction, students and the instructor work together. Communication goes two ways.[1]

Amongst the *presentation formats* are:

○　lectures;

○　student presentations (in which a student reports on the outcomes of an assignment, for example);

○　demonstrations (such as performing a chemical experiment in front of the students);

○　audio-visual presentations (films, tapes, TV programmes etc.).

The presentation format is often suitable for the purpose of introducing new areas of knowledge, as well as for relating and systematizing what has been taught. It is common, however, that instructors rely one-sidedly on presentation formats due to the force of habit or overly optimistic confidence in the power of straightforward transmission of knowledge.

Independent assignment formats include:

o   tests or exams;

o   independent exercises or application tasks (without help from the instructor);

o   assigned reading or viewing tasks;

o   programmed instruction or instruction through the use of other "self-guiding" learning materials (including many forms of computer-aided instruction);

o   complex independent tasks, such as research projects and projects of practical or artistic production.

Independent assignments are presented to students in the form of tasks. *Student tasks* are often particularly well suited for motivating students to tackle new subject matter, as well as for practising, applying, controlling and evaluating what has been taught. Instruction through student tasks is decisively important for developing independent activity on the part of the learners. Nevertheless, student tasks are commonly used inconsiderately, as a mere change from the prevailing presentation type of teaching. In this case they risk to be rather ambiguous and have no accurate directions or clear instructional aim.

Lecturer M. M. has spoken for an hour on newly proposed laws on workplace safety and health. He notices that the participants are tired and decides to lighten up the atmosphere by means of group work. He gives them the task to "consider the effects of the proposed legislation on the activities of regional factory inspectorates".

One of the participants asks how the results of the group work will be reported and evaluated. M. M. says that a reporter should be chosen in each group to write down the ideas kindled during the discussion and to orally summarize them afterwards. He gives no criteria regarding evaluation.

M. M.'s approach won't do. In order to make teaching through student tasks constructive, the instructor must carefully think over the reasons for using tasks and the kinds of mental and practical work they require.

Teaching is the direction and guidance of the *learners' activity*. Activity manifests itself in the performance and completion of tasks. In order to be constructive, learning must be built around a *series of tasks* which are meaningful to the learners.

To create meaningful student tasks, we need to reconsider what we mean by a task. Newman, Griffin and Cole point out that in school instruction tasks are commonly given in such a form that their goals are predefined by the teacher. Such tasks are not *"whole tasks"* because they preclude goal formation on the part of the student.

"In everyday situations people are not always presented with clearly stated goals. They often have to figure out what the problem is, what the constraints are, as well as how to solve the problem once they have formulated it. In other words, in everyday situations people are confronted with the 'whole' task."[2]

If only partial tasks, with predetermined goals, are given to students, the students will reinterpret them in any case. Thus, the meaning of the task is different for the students and for the teacher. The teacher does not know how the students interpret the task.

In instructional settings, the whole task, including joint goal formation, can be accomplished through negotiation between the teacher and the students. Therefore the actual performance or solution of the task should be preceded by a phase of cooperative negotiation and formulation of the task.

For the construction of meaningful whole tasks, the decisive precondition is the *inclusion of context in the task*. In work-related adult training, this means above all that tasks should be found in real work settings, genuine communities of practice. Many tasks can actually be performed and solved in such real life settings. Many others must be simulated, reconstructed in classrooms or special workshops. The crucial criterion is that students are able to construct the task as part of a work activity, not being forced to tackle the task as an isolated exercise.

Such contextually embedded tasks are demanding to identify and design. A wise instructor creates a *student task bank* where task descriptions, their instructions, criteria for evaluation, and samples of solutions are stored for continuous use and improvement.

The possibilities for using student tasks are not limited to practising and applying new knowledge. They can be used to induce all the steps of the cycle of investigative learning. The purpose of student tasks in connection with motivation is to tune into a cognitive conflict, to show up the insufficiency of students' former knowledge and skills. During orientation they are aimed at the formation of an orientation basis.

The actual assignments, or instructions for performance, are very important in the use of learner tasks. The nature of the task must be made clear to the students. Often the most sensible thing is to formulate written instructions in order to avoid ambiguity and errors of interpretation. Instructions should show what tools might be used. In tasks which serve the acquisition of new knowledge, practice or application, it is particularly important to indicate how the orientation basis is to be used as an aid: may students have it in front of them, or should they have internalized it and resort to the mental model? Similarly clear should be the form of collaboration and interaction required between students in the different phases of the task.

A series of student tasks should include different types of problems for which the solutions are to be based on the same principle. This is important in order to assure the applicability and flexibility of the orientation basis to be acquired.

The difficulty of a student task depends to a great extent on three factors:

o   A task is easier when the orientation basis is materially at hand as an external help. The task usually becomes more difficult when it must be solved with the help of an internalized model.

o   A task is easier to accomplish when its contents are familiar. It becomes more difficult when the same principle is applied to something unknown.

o   Generally, tasks serving the transmission and systematization of new information are easier than tasks designed for problem solving. Usually the most difficult tasks are those which require constructive, creative application of what has been learnt in the generation of novel analyses or products.

The concept of "difficulty" is commonly associated with negative con-notations. It is thought that difficult tasks should be avoided if teaching is to succeed. However, it has been shown that the most successful teachers use notably more difficult tasks than others. They demand a lot of their students. This means that they make their instruction challenging and interesting. They also give more support and guidance to their students than their less success-ful colleagues. One of the main reasons for poor learning results is instruction which is made too simple, instruction in which students are not given tasks which require them to employ their faculties and develop their abilities.[3]

Difficulty is a completely different matter from instruction which advances too quickly. Instruction can be made artificially difficult and painful by giving too little time to accomplish a task. Similarly, difficulty involves something different from unclarity or poor directions. Instruction can like-wise be made artificially difficult by constructing a faulty or superficial orien-tation basis, by giving students unclear directions, or by hindering cooperation or debate between them. These artificial difficulties do not agree with teacher ethics. High demands also require that the instructor respects and carefully guides the students.

Formats of cooperative instruction may include the following:

o   instructional questioning;

o   instructional discussion (exchange or negotiation of opinions, ideas or experiences);

o   joint exercise or application (with the instructor along as a guide or a participant);

o   brainstorming sessions and similar specific techniques for joint production of ideas;

o   complex joint performances (for example, of artistic productions).

Cooperative instruction is often a suitable format for motivating and orienting students to new subject matter, and for systematizing, controlling and evaluating what has been learnt. Class discussion, for example, can be used effectively to categorize subject matter and to focus attention on key issues and eventually unclear or poorly defined areas of the contents. However, class discussion is often held as an absolute value in itself and allowed to get muddled and haphazard.

Joint exercises, joint application tasks and complex joint performances are student tasks just like the student tasks within the format of independent assignments. The difference is that in joint tasks the instructor is actively involved as a mentor, facilitator or participant.

Social modes

By social modes, we mean the manner in which participants are grouped and their interaction is organized. The most common social mode is the traditional *frontal classroom teaching* in which a whole group, typically 20 to 40 students but occasionally much more, work in the same space under the guidance and immediate control of a teacher.

The opposite of frontal teaching is the *individual work* students do on their own apart from the learning group, in a separate room for instance. Most homework is usually done in this way.

A third social mode is *work in small groups*, usually comprised of anywhere from three to eight students working on a common task. A formal division of labor is not necessary, though a chairperson and reporter might be named. The group works as a whole, often rather spontaneously.

A less common social mode is *work in pairs*. It can have certain advantages over small group work, especially if the pairs are made up of individuals whose points of view and tools of knowledge are different enough to produce fruitful tension and sociocognitive conflict. Work in pairs generally requires less time than small group study. The time required to get accustomed to and to feel one's way with the partner is lesser than in small groups. On the other hand, there is less variety of viewpoints and intellectual resources available.

Sectional work is also a social mode. It refers to the division of a learning group into two or more fairly large groups or "sections", typically consisting of ten or more students. Each section is given a rather large and complex task requiring internal organization and division of labour. This social mode is not used very often, due to its demanding nature. But it may be particularly appropriate for tasks which simulate real complex situations; it obliges participants to project themselves into the problems of cooperation and planning of work.

Social modes and instructional formats are two different and relatively independent external dimensions of instructional methods. But they easily get confused with one another. For example, it is often thought that a lecture is a method of frontal classroom teaching for large groups. In other words, a lecture (a presentation format of instruction) is identified with frontal teaching for whole groups (a social mode). This needlessly limits innovative variation and elasticity. A lecture, for instance, may also be suitable for a small group. Often it is also used in individual mentoring; this is work in a pair in which the instructor is the second party.

Instructional functions

The purpose of teaching is to achieve high quality learning. In chapter 2 of this book we explained what is meant by productive and investigative learning. Such learning takes the form of a multi-step cycle. By what he or she does, the instructor can deeply influence whether or not students manage to proceed in their learning efforts through meaningfully interconnected steps and thoroughly accomplish each one.[4]

In order to do this, the instructor must be aware of the function of each phase of his or her teaching from the point of view of the students' learning process. The instructor must ask: "At this stage, am I attempting to construct an orientation basis with my students – or to systematize and consolidate what I have already taught to them – or perhaps motivate them to embark on an entirely new topic?" The instructor has reason to worry if he or she cannot explain the function of each phase.

Nine different instructional functions can be distinguished:

1. *Preparing*. This means priming students for a new thematic unit by establishing its importance in practice and its connection with what has been learnt earlier. This function also includes social and organizational preparations, such as introducing the participants and familiarizing the students with the practical arrangements of the course.

2. *Motivating*. This means arousing the interest of students in the new thematic unit by giving rise to a problem, by creating a cognitive conflict. This happens by confronting students with meaningful and important tasks from

the practice, tasks in which their former concepts and ways of working are shown to be mistaken or insufficient.

3. *Orientating*. This means formulating the cognitive objective of the thematic unit, that is, constructing its orientation basis. It can be worked out together with the students in search for solutions and explanatory models for the motivational task and cognitive conflict. The core idea or general principle of the thematic unit is sketched in the form of simplified models. The orientation basis can also be developed and completed as instruction advances. In other words, the orientation function may be repeated during various phases of the thematic unit.

4. *Conveying and elaborating new knowledge*. This means "filling out" and enriching the orientation basis with adaptations, specifics and variations. New knowledge can be conveyed and elaborated by using different instructional formats – not just presentations. At its best, the elaboration of new knowledge is an active process of finding, discovering, structuring and interpreting new data with the help of the orientation basis as an explanatory model.

5. *Systematizing*. Here one returns to the essential points of the thematic unit, recapitulating and highlighting the most important junctures. One aims at clear organization of what has been taught. Even after careful orientation, new subject matter is often fuzzy like porridge for the students. For this reason restful breaks are necessary during which students may check their memory or present questions. In this way they are helped to separate the essential from the unessential, to identify points which remained unclear to them, and to recognize inner connections and relations between various items in the subject matter. Again, this function can be achieved by means of many different instructional formats and social modes.

6. *Practising*. This is the development of knowledge into skills, or the transformation of subject matter into the student's preparedness for action. The goal is to master specific performances and operations. Acquiring a smooth skill typically requires numerous repetitions of the performance with the help of an external model and then without it. Practice does not only pertain to practical skills, it is also needed for learning to use new concepts and to affirm mental skills. Often a course is too short to provide for extensive amounts of practice. However, it is important that key skills are initially practised under critical supervision and in connection to the broader theoretical and conceptual orientation basis from which they are derived. Practising a skill often brings to light misconceptions and gaps in students' learning. Thus, while this function mainly serves internalization, it is also important as a means of externalizing, making observable, the mental models acquired by the students.

7. *Applying*. This means solving novel tasks with the help of the new orientation basis. Evaluative (analytical) application can be distinguished

from constructive (synthetic) application. Evaluative application refers to the appraisal and analysis of some object, phenomenon, or text with the help of the newly acquired model or principle. Constructive application means the production of something entirely new, for instance the creation of an organizational or technological solution. In practice, these two forms of application are often closely connected. In a demanding project, the students must often first analyse and define a problem (evaluative application), then produce a solution to it (constructive application).

Often practising precedes applying in that the mastery of certain rudimentary operations is necessary before more creative applications can be accomplished. On the other hand, applying may also come first, for example when a novel solution is first invented and subsequently turned into practical operations by means of repeated trials.

8. *Criticizing*. This means that the students are invited to evaluate the subject matter, the explanatory power and usefulness of its orientation basis: Does the knowledge they are studying provide tools for mastering the practice? What are its strengths and limitations?

9. *Evaluating and controlling*. The instructor assesses students' learning and students are led to assess and correct their own learning. Students are to ask: What have I and my group understood? What can I and my group do thanks to what we learned – and what did we fail to learn? How did I and my group study? What are the weak and strong points of our work? What learning strategies did we use?

The instructor uses means of evaluation and control to develop a conscious ability in students to monitor and evaluate their own performance. By the same means, the instructor obtains information about the quality and results of his or her teaching. The correction of lacunas and mistakes and the rectifying and guidance of the learning process are directly connected to control.

However, control techniques, such as tests, are often used unwisely. They are used to awaken instrumental motivation in students and to rank them continuously with abstract scales that have little to do with deep understanding and mastery of practice. Examinations and tests too often measure the number of correct answers students produce rather than how they understand subject matter or their ability to apply creatively what they have learned.

Particularly in work-related training of adults, a careful follow-up of exercises and application tasks tells a lot more about a student's learning than the results from a multiple choice test. In the assessment of learning results, there are good reasons for using techniques of qualitative evaluation more courageously. Such techniques might include students writing journals of their understanding of the central ideas during the course, portfolios of products of the students' work, application tasks in which students must not only find solutions but also explain how they arrived at them. A qualitative evaluation can be begun by giving the "correct answer" to the students and then asking them to give arguments for and against the answer. Often videotaping students' performance and analysing the tape together with the students reveals crucial weaknesses and innovative solutions better than paper and pencil tests.[5]

Complete instructional treatment

The nine instructional functions characterized above are not a list that the teacher should go through mechanically and in that order in every curriculum unit. On the other hand, it would not be sufficient to impulsively choose amongst them whatever seems good.

In fact, these instructional functions are only meaningful when they form a whole. This whole is called *complete instructional treatment* of a thematic unit.

In traditional schooling, the dominant pattern of teaching was based on the singular, isolated lesson as the unit of instruction. A typical lesson was begun with teacher questions aimed at controlling the acquisition and memorization of the contents the previous lesson. Next, the teacher would present a carefully measured portion of new knowledge. At the end, there would be exercises based on the new knowledge. This simple pattern was repeated time and again.

According to the view of learning adopted in this book, the purpose of complete instructional treatment is to ensure the completion of a cycle of investigative learning in each thematic unit (see Chapter 2, diagrams 7 and 8). Instructional functions are teachers' means for evoking and achieving steps in the cycle of investigative learning. Diagram 21 illustrates the correspondence between instructional functions and learning steps.

In real instructional practice, there is never a full correspondence between what the teacher aims at and what actually happens in students' learning. There is always a degree of indeterminacy and mismatch between teaching and learning. The teacher may aim at systematizing knowledge already taught – but the students may step forward and turn the situation into critique of the contents. Or the teacher may want to engage the students into applying the new orientation basis in novel tasks – but the students are not ready and they step back to re-orientate themselves, to reconstruct the orientation basis once again.

The instructor should plan and carry through the teaching of a thematic unit so that instructional functions are used in a flexible and versatile way, to achieve a complete investigative learning cycle. There is no universally correct

Diagram 21: Instructional functions and corresponding learning steps

Instructional functions (used by the teacher)	Learning steps (performed by the students)
• Preparing	
• Motivating	• Motivation
• Orienting	• Orientation
• Conveying and elaborating new knowledge	• Internalization
• Systematizing	• Internalization
• Practising	• Internalization/externalization
• Applying	• Externalization
• Criticizing	• Critique
• Evaluating and controlling	• Control

order for or time distribution between instructional functions. In a thematic unit, one and the same instructional function may be repeated several times, while another function may be left aside.

Faulty treatment leads to superficial learning. Complete instructional treatment is essential if knowledge is to come alive and be applicable.

Complete instructional treatment means that students, working through tasks, "give birth" themselves to the central ideas and concepts of the thematic unit. These must be instruments for solving real problems.

It is important that the explanatory model, the orientation basis, is used for accomplishing new and different tasks. It is not enough that concepts are shaped as means for solving standard problems. One must learn to use them to formulate, explain and solve new problems.

Complete instructional treatment in practice

Heinz Grassel and Regina Bonnke compared how schoolteachers with good and schoolteachers with poor learning outcomes used various instructional functions and to what extent they realized a complete instructional treatment. They noted the following differences:

Good teachers used on average five instructional functions in each lesson; less successful teachers used three or four.

The better teachers used noticeably more time to orientate students to new subject matter. They gave them preliminary information with which students could quickly understand the essential points and then used it as support in the form of diagrams and models.

The better teachers recapitulated and made summaries of the essential points of the topic much more often than the weaker teachers.

The better teachers were not content with one task for each topic; they gave students several interconnected tasks for the same thematic unit (a combination or a series of tasks). The better teachers preferred difficult and demanding tasks. But they also guided the students in carrying them out much more than the other teachers and resorted repeatedly to such means as orientative diagrams.

The better teachers trained their students to control and evaluate their own ability already before doing exercises. More attentively than their colleagues, they also followed how the students solved these tasks, and not just the final outcomes.[6]

Ritva Jakku-Sihvonen conducted a study of the instruction given in state employees' training courses in Finland. Her results showed that only about 30 per cent of the training sessions started with an orientative introduction to the subject. In 78 per cent of the sessions there was no practical exercise at all. Systematization of the contents was almost always absent. And attempts to control and evaluate what was learned could only be observed in 20 per cent of the sessions. Unrivalled attention was given to transmitting new knowledge and associating it with former knowledge.

The researcher herself commented: "Based on the frequency of instructional functions, one is left with the general impression that instructors strongly emphasize the presentation and, to some extent, the consolidation of knowledge. Goal-orientation seems to be shoved into the background, as is also practical action directed at mastering course contents. Obviously, then, the intention within the teaching process is good learning, but its achievement is reduced to the transmission of knowledge rather than the pursuit of actually mastering it."[7]

Complete instructional treatment is a demanding standard for instructors. Ideally it should be carried out in each thematic unit. Complete instructional treatment helps to guarantee the integral learning of each unit and to create a firm basis from which to move forward to the following topic.

The complete instructional treatment is facilitated by having plenty of time for a thematic unit. However, there are situations in which one must simply be content with a single teaching lesson or lecture, perhaps lasting just one hour. Even such an isolated lesson can include several instructional functions which together form an entire unit, though in that case one runs the risk of treating the subject matter superficially and switching too quickly from one function to another.

A lesson of an hour's duration need not be limited to the transmission of new knowledge. Lecturers can motivate and orientate participants to their topic. They should also systematize the essential aspects of the topic, for example by means of selected questions and discussion. A carefully prepared lecturer might append some small form of practice and application to a short lecture. On the basis of responses from the audience, he or she might also control and correct the results of their learning. In other words, some restricted form of complete instructional treatment can in principle be realized even in one lesson. But to do it successfully is difficult and requires meticulous planning. Thus, this should be regarded as an exception, not something to be striven after.

There are also exceptional curriculum units for which it is neither possible nor necessary to apply the standard of complete instructional treatment. This might be the case in an introduction unit or in a concluding unit of a course. In the introduction, one might concentrate on preparing, motivating and orientating. In the conclusion, one might be intensely systematizing, criticizing, evaluating and controlling. In such units, one can intentionally aim at a *partial instructional treatment*.

The use of complete instructional treatment is not limited to the level of thematic units. The whole course must also be shaped to facilitate a meaningful and integral learning process. In other words, thematic units should be connected to each other and progress logically. Each unit will have its own *main instructional function* when viewed as a part of a course. Certain thematic units primarily convey and elaborate new knowledge, others focus on applying it.

On the one hand, then, the thematic unit needs complete instructional treatment; on the other hand, the whole course needs it as well. The thematic units are the foundation, however. The quality of learning depends on the complete instructional treatment carried out in each one of them.

Analysing instruction

Suppose that this book is given to a student to read in preparation for a forthcoming course. This student has done some training, now he or she wants to get better in that job. The student knows that in the beginning of the course a test will be held on the basis of the book. The student reads the book at home or in the workplace.

How should we analyse this sequence of instruction using the concepts presented in this chapter? What instructional formats, social modes and instructional functions are involved?

Diagram 22: Form for planning and analysing instruction

Course: Training of trainers – New approach to instruction

Thematic unit and its main function in the course (1)	Period (2)	Time (3)	Contents (4)	Instructional function (5)	Instructional format (6)	Social mode (7)	Materials, instruments (8)	Notes, observations (9)
1. Introduction	1.1	about 5 days	The book *Training for change*, its central ideas	– motivating, – orienting	– independent assignment: reading task (student task #1)	– individual work	– book	
	1.2	30 min (20)	Opening of course – Introduction of participants	– preparing	– student presentations	– frontal		
		(10)	– Course programme	– preparing	– lecture	– frontal	– copies of programme	
	1.3	45 min	Test: three essay questions requiring use of key concepts of book	– motivating, – evaluating and controlling	– independent assignment: writing task (student task #2)	– individual work	– students may use the book	– students choose the location of work
	1.4	45 min	Student answers; Contents of the book	– evaluating and controlling – motivating	– questioning and discussion	– frontal		– students correct their own papers
	1.5	15 min	Task instructions: Fill in the model of investigative learning (diagram 8) with specific contents describing your own training work	– orienting	– lecture – demonstration	– frontal	– imaginary trainer used as an example	
	1.6	40 min	Task completion; see above	– orienting – applying	– independent assignment (student task #3)	– work in pairs	– outcomes on paper in diagram form	

Diagram 22 is a form which can be used to analyse and plan instruction. The example chosen here is the beginning of a course for trainers, aimed at developing an instructional approach based on similar ideas as the ones presented in this book.

It is natural when analysing teaching to advance from the readily observable external aspects to the internal aspects, that is from instructional formats and social modes to instructional functions. It will be recalled that instructional functions cannot usually be specified without outlining the complete treatment of a thematic unit and the significance of each teaching phase as an intermediate step.

In the example analysed in diagram 22, the reading of the book is aimed at arousing a conflict between the reader's former concepts and teaching habits and the new points of view in the book: this is motivating. At the same time, the book is supposed to promote the formation of a new orientation basis: this is orientating. Here we see a phase of teaching with two equally important parallel functions – a twin function. In diagram 22, there are other examples of such twin functions.

Each teaching phase also has its side effects, secondary functions. But the teacher must concentrate in his or her planning and analysis on specifying the *main function* of each phase from the point of view of complete instructional treatment.

The form depicted in diagram 22 also includes a column for notes. When teaching is analysed, this column is the place for observations on particular characteristics of the instructional sequence, including weaknesses, disturbances and innovative solutions.

The uses of the form (diagram 22) in the planning of instruction are discussed in detail in Chapter 7.

The choice of teaching methods

The ideas presented in this chapter can now be condensed into a few simplified directions for choosing teaching methods:

Stage 1. When drawing up your orientation basis, clarify to yourself what is the "red thread" of the contents of this thematic unit and the logic of the subject matter. That is, draw up a preliminary scheme of the succession of main points and essential concepts.

Stage 2. Reshape this scheme into a draft or synopsis for complete instructional treatment of the thematic unit. The contents must be divided into phases and the instructional function of each phase must be specified so that they all form a sequence that makes possible the completion of an integral cycle of investigative learning. Be careful not to neglect any of the six steps of the cycle of investigative learning. Use and combine instructional functions with elasticity and imagination.

Stage 3. Choose the most meaningful instructional format and social mode for each instructional function. Maintain variety. Remember that external factors are also important. Sitting in one place for too long a time and staring at the same faces also renders learning difficult even when the contents of teaching are inspiring and demanding.

Stage 4. Carefully outline the student tasks you intend to use in the different phases. Try to construct a series of tasks with varying degrees of complexity. Aim at whole tasks that are embedded in the context of the relevant work practice. Remember that a thematic unit with no student tasks is probably ineffective and boring. Still worse is a unit in which the orientation basis is of no use in mastering the student tasks.

---

[1] Cooperative instruction refers here to two-way interaction between the teacher and the students. It must be distinguished from theories and programmes of collaborative learning which refer to collaboration between students. See footnote 29 in Chapter 2.

[2] Newman, Griffin & Cole, 1989, p. 33. On problem finding, see also Getzels & Csikszentmihalyi (1976); on the students' interpretation of tasks, see Hallden (1982).

[3] See for example Zankov et al. (1977).

[4] Researchers are often sceptical about whether teachers can make a difference in the quality of student learning. Probably one reason for this is that the multi-step cycle of investigative learning is institutionally difficult to implement in school settings which operate within the traditional framework of enclosed classrooms, discrete lessons, and separate subjects or disciplines. These boundaries are much less prevalent in work-related training of adults.

[5] For methods of video-based analysis of work, see Jordan & Henderson (1993).

[6] Grassel & Bonnke, 1977, pp. 192-199.

[7] Jakku-Sihvonen, 1981, pp. 81-83.

PLANNING INSTRUCTION

7

The importance of planning

What is the most common way to plan teaching? In work-related training of adults, one often proceeds as follows:

Administrative planning for a training session starts when a course is deemed necessary and given some general title. The schedule, location, lecture themes and possible lecturers are determined, and the procedures for selecting participants are decided. A brief introduction to the course might be drawn up with apparently convincing behavioural objectives.

Specific planning of teaching only begins when the date for the session is drawing near. It is done in a hurry, with much less care than the administrative planning. Lecturers are either invited for a joint consultation or contacted individually regarding the subject on which they intend to speak. With luck, they provide a skeleton of their lectures just before the course or after it has begun. By this stage, the planner of the course, normally the same person as its director, is pretty worried that the presentations will overlap. Usually he or she does not venture to interfere too much with lecture contents – after all, the lecturers are specialists in their fields. Nor would he or she have time for that.

Planners or course directors are also concerned to make the instruction agreeable. They place group work and breaks between heavy lectures. They invent some original sources of variety, perhaps a film, a panel discussion or a field trip. They also plan how the different lectures will be connected to each other, sketching out ways to introduce the individual lecturers. Finally, they plan an opening for the session ("Should a management representative be invited to make a few opening remarks?") and a conclusion ("Don't forget to have participants fill out evaluation forms to ascertain which lecturers were good").

The planner or course director might in fact give instructions to the lecturers, for example: "Use clear overhead projector transparencies," or "One hears poorly in the back of the room, so speak loudly enough." These instructions generally concern the way in which contact is made with the audience.

How can the planning described above be characterized? It was concentrated on and limited to the *external factors of instruction*. Diagram 23 reiterates this book's view of the external and internal factors in teaching. The focus of this chapter, the output of planning, is highlighted in italics.

Diagram 23: The external and internal factors in teaching (3)

External factors (means by which students' observable behaviour and situation are controlled)	Internal factors (means by which students' mental work is guided)
Instructional objectives	
desired observable performances described in the form of behavioural objectives	contents to be mastered, described in the form of cognitive objectives, or orientation bases of performances
Study motivation	
stimuli, rewards and punishments to keep the attention of the students	students' interest in the subject matter awakened through intellectual confrontation and cognitive conflict
Choice of teaching content	
ready-made facts and performance schemes	models, principles, systems of ideas, and modes of discourse
Methods of teaching	
variable forms of teaching; entertainment; maintenance of momentary alertness; assurance of students' external activeness	stepwise realization of an entire cycle of learning by means of complete instructional treatment
Output of planning	
time schedule, lecture outline, transparencies	*curriculum for a thematic unit of instruction, explaining the progress of teaching from the viewpoint of learning*
The instructor in the teaching situation (teaching skills)	
presentation skills; command of immediate social interaction; organizational skills; audiovisual techniques	command of the content of the subject matter; flexible reliance on the curriculum; instructor's ethics

Planning which concentrates on the external factors of teaching basically produces time schedules, lecture outlines and packages of material, for instance, for the overhead projector. It does not provide a design which outlines the *learning process of students*.

Individual lecturers' or instructors' plans for teaching are also often limited to the external factors. They plan their lectures as if for themselves alone, dishing out ready information to students without referring to the key concepts of their subject matter or to the sources of the conclusions they draw. Instead of on learning, they focus on "creating contact", "making an impact" or "arresting attention".

Thus they develop stylish, multi-coloured diagrams or clever quips to make their lectures spicy, thinking they have succeeded when they get participants laughing. Or perhaps they put their main emphasis on discussion and develop social techniques to inspire even the most taciturn students to speak their mind – thus avoiding the burden of teaching anything new to the students.

Many instructors are familiar with the temptation not to plan their teaching at all. They simply present the audience with what they know (or have read) of a subject and "improvise" the rest.

Improvisation, sensitivity and instinctive mastery of the situation are often held to be the most important distinctions of a good teacher. It is said that teaching is an art which cannot be nor should be overly planned in advance. Advance planning is thought to bind the teacher, to make teaching formal and lifeless.

This is a prejudiced understanding. Improvisation and planning are not antithetic. On the contrary, it is difficult to improvise without a carefully drawn plan. If a plan is missing, teaching is almost sure to be stiff and schematic: one begins to repeat oneself, tell the same anecdotes, use the same drawings, without thinking how they all connect.

A careful preliminary plan gives a firm basis on which instructors know they may improvise when need and opportunity arise. Without a good plan, unanticipated situations are likely to confuse the lecturer's pre-arranged ideas. Intensive discussion might arise around some particular detail and suddenly the lecturer notices that the time is up and the main point has not been treated. This is not improvising or being flexible, but rather being adrift.

The instructor who has drawn up a detailed plan of the unit, on the other hand, can proportion the unanticipated situation with regards to the whole. This instructor can re-estimate the use of time in order to make sure that the main point of the unit receives sufficient attention. But only a plan which is based on the students' learning process can have this practical value. A plan for teaching is needed which starts with the *internal factors of teaching*.

The concept of curriculum

Planning is not merely thinking in advance about instruction. It requires the drawing up of a written plan. Such a plan is called a *curriculum*.

Traditionally curricula have been designed for studies leading to a degree or diploma, such as is given in high schools or trade schools. Courses of work-related adult education or personnel training often do not lead to a formal degree or diploma. This means larger degrees of freedom and innovation in planning – not less need for planning.

A curriculum is aimed at guiding and monitoring the teaching and learning processes. For a plan to be really useful and not formal, the persons who will be carrying out the teaching must be centrally involved in the design. It must be the instructors' own plan for guiding their work, not obligations or limitations set by someone else. Even if there is no curriculum drawn up for the whole course, it is beneficial for the individual lecturer to have prepared a plan for his or her own teaching portion.

Curriculum fuses administrative planning of a course with the design of the teaching-learning process proper. In a sense, the administrative and economic specifications of training are translated into the language of teaching and learning. Curriculum design, however, should definitely not be subordinated to administrative planning. On the contrary, the instructional concerns which manifest themselves in the preparation of curriculum should also influence decisions concerning the duration and location of training and the selection of participants.

A curriculum serves the following purposes:

○ A curriculum guides and coordinates the work of instructors. It helps the individual teacher to harmonize his or her own teaching with the whole course.

○ A curriculum provides teachers with a shared language and toolkit for planning. The use of a common model for planning a curriculum facilitates communication between instructors and increases their collaboration concerning contents and methods.

○ A curriculum promotes the development of continuous, multi-phased training programmes and multifaceted organizational forms for teaching and learning. The preparation of a curriculum implies a desire to encourage integral learning and thorough teaching. A curriculum permits the association of several different, successive or parallel portions of training such as courses, seminars, theme days, self-instruction, mentoring and apprenticeship in the workplace, and study groups.

○ A curriculum promotes the documenting and practical discussion of teaching experiences as well as the systematic evaluation of teaching. A written, precise curriculum is a document which can be effectively exploited in teacher training. The valuable accomplishments, eventual difficulties and new insights concerning specific points of a curriculum can be consciously and systematically documented in the process and at the conclusion of teaching.

o   A curriculum orientates and prepares students for instruction. It can and should be given to students to be used as a tool for reflecting on the studies and for participating in their continuous design, critique and evaluation.

o   A curriculum facilitates complete instructional treatment and integral investigative learning. A detailed, theoretically informed plan which seeks to monitor the teaching-learning process is the only guarantee of complete instructional treatment.

o   A curriculum increases teachers' sensitivity, accuracy and flexibility. A written curriculum gives them the possibility to occasionally disengage themselves in the midst of teaching to spend a moment in dialogue with their curriculum. This prevents instructors from getting carried away by situational stimulation and from admiring too much the sound of their own voices. Appropriate improvisation is only possible when the whole plan is mastered.

The general part of a curriculum

The curriculum can be divided into two parts, the general and the specific. Both have their own purposes.

The general part of a curriculum gives an overall picture of the background of the training course or program, its aims, contents, and the manner in which it will be carried out. The general part may include the following components:

1. A description of the competencies which are to be gained by training.

For example:
The purpose of this course is to train new factory inspectors who master the legislation on workplace safety and health and know how to apply it by taking independent and collaborative actions and decisions that facilitate safety and health in workplaces.

2. A comment on how the training is linked to the development of the work practice and organization.

For example:
This training is concerned with enhancing the transformation of factory inspectors' work practice and organization from the traditional "police" role toward the role of a consultant (This may be concretized with the help of a model, such as diagram 9 in Chapter 2.)

3. An account of the basis for selecting participants and the possibilities for further training.

For example:
Participants should have completed basic courses in hazard identification, accident prevention and industrial hygiene before this course.

An extension course will be organized for participants within a year. At that time, practical experiences of applying the contents of the present course will be presented and evaluated.

4. A comment on the selection of contents.

For example:
The bases for selecting course contents have been (a) the rapid changes in work conditions due to new technologies and globalization of production, (b) new experiences gained in various countries from preventive and developmental approaches to occupational safety and health.

5. A statement on the cognitive objectives of training.

For example:
The objective of the course is to develop the ability of trainees to understand and master practically the complex system of factors affecting workplace safety and health. This complex system is presented in a diagrammatic form (see diagram 16 in Chapter 4).

On the basis of the systemic view, the trainees will also learn to select and use flexibly key practical procedures and classifications needed in factory inspections (see diagrams 17 and 18 as examples).

6. A statement concerning the general principles of instruction.

For example:
The following principles will be observed in the course:

○   instruction will advance through problematic case studies; participants will be given abundant tasks and intensive individual and group work will be required of them;

○   conceptual models will be continuously applied and elaborated in the tasks.

7. A comment on organizational arrangements.

For example:
Instruction will take place during a five-day residential course. Before the course begins, students will perform a preliminary task and their solutions will be reported during the course. At the beginning, students will be divided

into four groups for solving the various tasks; the groups will remain the same throughout the course. A special feedback day will be linked to the course.

8. A list of thematic units.

For example:
The course will be divided into the following thematic units:

(i)   Introduction

(ii)   The origin and development of factory inspection

(iii) The system of factors influencing workplace safety and health

(iv)   Practical procedures and classifications in consultative factory inspection

(v)   Course summary

(vi)   Feedback day

Thus the general part of a curriculum reflects the instructional approach of an entire course, the "philosophy" behind it, so to speak. The general part of a curriculum for a course of just a few days' duration might be less extensive. For a longer training programme, it might contain a more ambitious analysis which reflects the evolution of the work practice of the target group and a detailed specification of the competence aimed for.

The specific part of a curriculum

The purpose of the specific or detailed part of a curriculum is to guide the processes of teaching and learning. How detailed the specific part of a curriculum is depends largely on the size of the whole course. Obviously it is not sensible to describe every minute of a course which will last several months or years. On the other hand, the instructor of each thematic unit can be required to draw up an exact plan for his or her own teaching.

For a short course, it is possible and often worthwhile to prepare a very detailed curriculum, down to the level of about every five to ten minutes. This does not mean that the instructor is bound to the clock. The purpose of such detailed planning is rather to simulate and imagine in advance the steps of the actual instructional process so concretely that the contingencies and surprises of the practical realization will be met with deeper insight and more flexible alternatives in mind.

The specific part of a curriculum consists of *thematic units*. Each thematic unit is designed around two components: the *orientation basis* and the *complete instructional treatment*.

The form for planning the complete instructional treatment was depicted in diagram 22 in Chapter 6. In that form, the contents and methods of the thematic unit are represented alongside each other in their temporal succession. A blank version of the form can be found at the end of the book as Annex 2.

In Column 1 we find the number and name of the *thematic unit*. Its main instructional function within the whole course is mentioned in parentheses.

Column 2 expresses the boundaries and numbers of the *teaching periods*. A period indicates a session of work, for example one lesson, which ends with a break or a rearrangement of the situation.

Column 3 shows the *time* allotted for each period and each instructional function. Especially in concise courses, separate time allotments should be made for each instructional function. This way the actual realization of each function will be realistically assessed. The time given for period 1.1. in diagram 22 is exceptionally long and inexact (about five days) because it concerns a preparatory student task to be performed at home.

Column 4 is a fairly precise indication of the *contents* of each phase and instructional function. This column contains what is traditionally put in the "lecture outline'. More than that, it should also contain fairly detailed descriptions of the assignments of student tasks.

Column 5 indicates the *instructional function* of each teaching phase. This column is decisive in planning and evaluating complete instructional treatment. Whether complete instructional treatment has been thoroughly prepared or not shows up right away in the fifth column.

In Column 6 the corresponding *instructional format* is indicated for each instructional function. However, one must bear in mind that the format can also change during the same function, and vice versa, the function can change while the same instructional format is maintained.

Column 7 indicates the *social mode* for each instructional function. Again, the social mode may change while the function remains the same, and vice versa.

Column 8 lists the *materials and instruments* needed in the various phases and instructional functions.

Column 9 is left for instructor's *notes*, specific reminders and observations that help the teacher anticipate and later evaluate the process.

The form enables the planner to move *vertically (in time)*, column by column, starting with the contents and instructional functions which represent the internal factors of instruction. On the other hand, the planner can and should also move *horizontally (in space)*, integrating contents, instructional functions, formats and modes into meaningful social situations of teaching and learning. This kind of two-dimensional planning is tremendously important mental preparation for an instructor.

Experience shows that filling in this kind of a blank form gives a certain posture and lucidity even to a short course. The use of a blank form may be difficult to begin with, but it soon becomes quicker and easier.

Phases of preparation for teaching

Preparation of a curriculum generally demands the cooperation of the course planner and the specialists teaching the various thematic units. The course planner may first sketch a rough draft of the general part of the curriculum. Then he or she might negotiate with the various thematic unit instructors to obtain from them the specific parts of the curriculum. Finally, the course planner weaves the different parts together and presents his or her own suggestions.

We might summarize the step-by-step process of planning as follows:

1. Establish a connection between the training and the development of the work practice and organization of the trainees. Characterize the competencies the course is meant to produce.

2. Characterize the bases for the selection of the instructional contents.

3. Draw up a general view of the principles to be observed in teaching and define the organizational arrangements to be used.

4. Define the cognitive objectives of the entire course, its overall orientation basis.

5. "Translate" the orientation basis into learning contents, that is, into a list of thematic units, and define the main function of each unit as part of the whole course.

6. Specify the general cognitive conflict motivating the whole course and how participants are to be tuned into it.

7. Work out an orientation basis for each thematic unit.

8. Specify the contents of each thematic unit (the column 4 of the form in diagram 22); at the same time give a profile to the complete instructional treatment of the unit by dividing it into instructional functions (the column 5 of the form).

9. Define the time required for each instructional function. Take particular care not to make functions and units too brief and pressured in terms of time.

10. Choose the appropriate instructional format and social mode for each instructional function (columns 5 and 7 of the form).

11. Make sure the thematic unit contains at least one contextually meaningful student task (whole task) which anchors the instruction in the work practice it serves.

12. Divide the curriculum unit (the thematic unit) into teaching periods; decide when there should be breaks, and check that the time schedule can realistically be followed.

To divide the planning of teaching into phases like these simplifies the task. However, in reality the plan takes shape in a less linear, iterative way. The planner moves forwards and backwards from one phase to another.

A sketchy or defective curriculum is better than no curriculum at all. Often phase seven (formulating the orientation basis of each thematic unit), for example, remains incomplete because of scanty resources. This does not in itself prevent good quality teaching. It may be rewarding to work out an orientation basis first for just one or two thematic units. Experiences gained from using them may inspire further elaboration of the curriculum.

TEACHING SKILL

8

External criteria of skilful teaching

What are the characteristics of skilful teaching?

Once again, a distinction must be made between the internal and external factors of teaching. Teachers are not skilful just because they are experts with regards to the external factors of teaching. Their teaching may be showy or pleasantly entertaining, but this is not enough.

The external factors of teaching skill include at least the following points:

o   presentation skills: the skill of using one's voice and gestures effectively, of establishing contact with the audience;

o   interpersonal skills: the ability to encourage students to state their opinions, to listen to them, to create an intensive group atmosphere and to use group dynamics in teaching;

o   organizational skills: the skill to keep a good rhythm between instructional work and rest periods, to use the physical set-up effectively, to vary teaching formats and social modes sufficiently;

o   competence with audio-visual media and information technology: the skill to plan for and use effectively technical instruments, ranging the blackboard and the overhead projector video and computer technologies.

These external factors of teaching skill are necessary and useful, but not sufficient. They are the "shell" of good teaching. What then are the internal factors, the substance of good teaching?

Internal criteria of skilful teaching

The first and most important internal factor of skilful teaching is a thorough knowledge of the contents of the subject matter. The quality of teaching depends ultimately on how successfully one uncovers the essential principles and key ideas of the topic. This only happens when the teacher puts her- or himself wholly into the content. Most important is not to pass on ready information as if one were transferring merchandise, but to aim at tracing knowledge to its source and finding applications for it.

Good teachers ask "Why?" They demand of themselves that they be able to explain developmentally what they teach, to trace it to its origination and to follow its evolution. They look for systemic relations and interdependencies in the subject matter. This first factor can be reduced to one question: How good an orientation basis is the teacher able to draw up for the thematic unit?

The second internal factor of teaching skill is to be able to plan instruction drawing on a consistent theoretical view of teaching and learning. Teaching is not only art and improvisation. Planning instruction does not merely imply technical arrangements, but the practical application of a theory of the teaching-learning process.

This second factor can also be reduced to one question: How well does the teacher design a complete instructional treatment of a topic?

The third internal factor of teaching skill concerns teacher ethics. A teacher influences students through his or her personality, by the manner in which he or she relates to subject matter and to students. The basic points of

Diagram 24: Internal and external criteria of teaching

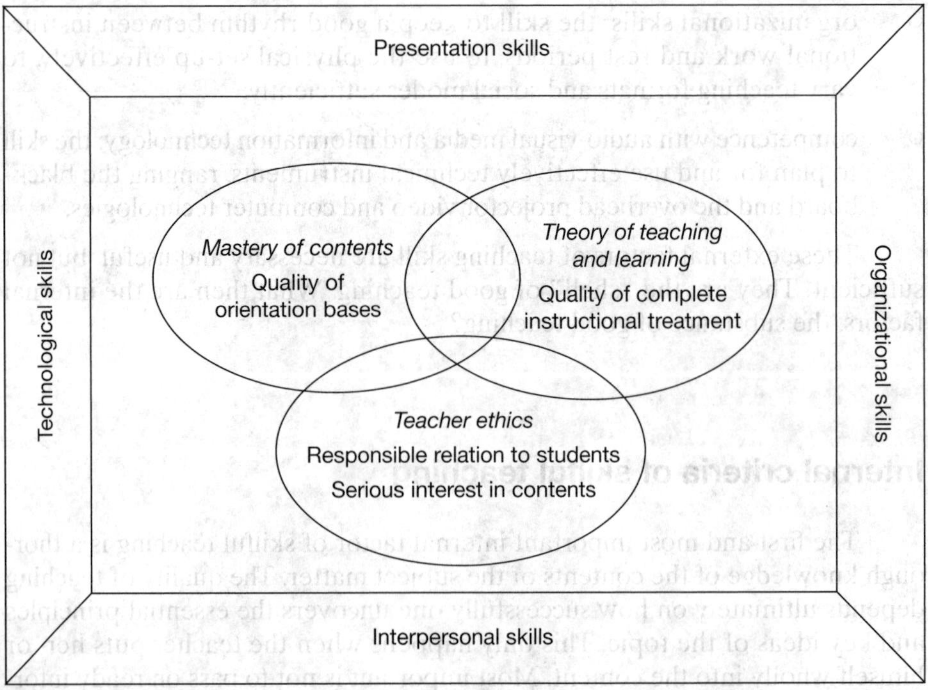

Presentation skills

Technological skills

Mastery of contents
Quality of orientation bases

Theory of teaching and learning
Quality of complete instructional treatment

Organizational skills

Teacher ethics
Responsible relation to students
Serious interest in contents

Interpersonal skills

teacher ethics are a demanding yet respectful relationship to students and a serious interest in the contents and uses of subject matter.

Teachers might know their subject and how to plan their teaching. But their skill is partial and their results uncertain if they relate to students with nonchalance or arbitrary favouritism. This also applies to an instructor who is not concerned if a student only pretends to understand a topic or who mocks and makes a fool of the student who fails.

Too much routine, getting set in one's ways and disappointment with poor results easily lead teachers to an ethically precarious position. They begin to explain that poor results are due to the "stupidity" or "laziness" of the students. Although these things might never be said openly, the students have a delicate instinct for such attitudes of teachers.

The same effect occurs if teachers take an indifferent attitude toward the contents of the material they are teaching. Students instinctively sense when teachers do not really stand behind the ideas they are teaching. The teacher's task is not to be a neutral medium of information who shies away from values and argumentation. Neutral teachers do not exist. Indifference itself implies an opinion.

Diagram 24 summarizes the external and internal criteria of teaching skill.

SUMMARY

9

Golden rules of teaching

The view of good instruction presented in this book can be condensed into a few "golden rules".

1. Cover less subject matter in your teaching, but teach it better and more thoroughly. One deeply understood and practically mastered idea or principle is more valuable than a hundred superficially learned fragments of knowledge.

2. Do not be content to teach "ready-made" decontextualized facts and skills. Always ask "why" and encourage students to do the same. Build up your teaching on the basis of general principles and powerful ideas found behind the factual details. Embed phenomena in practices and treat them as part of a system. Search for the origins and development of systems.

3. Evoke in the students a substantive motivation, an interest in the use value of the subject matter. Search for inner contradictions in practices and in knowledge. Use these as sources of sociocognitive conflicts, aroused by means of problems and challenging tasks which show students that their former knowledge and ways of working are insufficient.

4. Draw up an orientation basis that reveals essential principles of the subject matter. Use the orientation basis as an intellectual tool in formulating and solving student tasks. Prepare the orientation basis in the form of simplified models which students will internalize gradually. Invite students into a search for and formulation of the orientation bases.

5. Aim at cycles of investigative learning, including the steps of motivation, orientation, internalization, externalization, critique, and control. Facilitate and guide this designing a complete instructional treatment for each thematic unit. Always be clear of what is the instructional function of each phase of your teaching, that is, what kind of mental work you intend the students to accomplish.

6. Plan your teaching with care. Prepare a curriculum. Compare your instruction continuously with your curriculum. Note successes and breakdowns as well as new insights. Do not hesitate to let your plans and experiences be known for the benefit of other educators. Find out what the others do.

7. Require a lot from students, but respect them as well. Stand behind your words – take what you teach seriously and form your own views about it.

GLOSSARY

Behavioural objectives on instruction. Objectives which specify the students' desired observable performances as end results of instruction. Behavioural objectives are supposed to be as specific and exact as possible, preferably indicating the acceptable performance in measurable terms. The problem with behavioural objectives is that the same external performances can be based on completely different internal models and cognitive constructs. When the objective only describes a specific external performance, teaching and learning will likely be planned so as to lead as directly as possible to that performance. The internal conditions of external performance will easily be disregarded, thus remaining narrow and superficial.

Cognitive objectives of instruction. Cognitive objectives describe those principles and constructs on the understanding of which external performances are to be built. They explicate the "red thread" and gist of the subject matter – what insight is to be attained through a course. A cognitive objective is expressed in the form of an orientation basis, a model which can be used as an internalized tool for generating and monitoring appropriate performances in changing conditions.

Collaboration. Collaboration between learners facilitates every step of the cycle of investigative learning. Instead of relying only on the teacher as source of guidance, students can motivate each other, orientate each other, etc. Debate and argumentation as well as help and support from each other are important aspects of collaboration. Three types of collaboration may be identified: coordination, cooperation and communication.

Community of practice. Skills and knowledge are manifested and evolved in relatively stable communities of practice, typically workplaces. Training that aims at teaching individuals separated from their communities of practice is often ineffective and leads to little improvement in the work practice. Investigative learning requires a learning community. This typically exceeds the limits of classroom, consisting of a network of work teams and training instructions.

Complete instructional treatment. Instructional functions are only meaningful when they are together and form a complete instructional treatment of a thematic unit. The purpose of complete instructional treatment is to ensure the completion of a cycle of investigative learning in each thematic unit. The instructor should plan and carry out the teaching unit so that instructional functions are used in a flexible and versatile way.

Contents of instruction. Instructional contents may be understood as cultural models and modes of discourse. Form of representation and type of organization are important dimensions of the contents of instruction.

Context. Investigative learning is embedded in a web of meaningful social relations, practical tasks and cultural artifacts. In different phases of the learning cycle, these may be mobilized toward criticism of existing practices and ideas (context of criticism), toward discovery of new concepts and models (context of discovery), or toward practical application of new models and concepts (context of application). Each context of learning has its own typical tools and methods.

Curriculum. A curriculum is aimed at guiding and monitoring the teaching and learning processes of a training course. It guides and coordinates the work of instructors, helping the individual teacher to synchronize his or her own teaching with the whole course. A curriculum provides teachers with a shared language and toolkit for planning. It orientates and prepares students for instruction. A carefully crafted curriculum facilitates complete instructional treatment and integral investigative learning.

Cycle of investigative learning. See learning cycle.

Empirical knowledge. Based on observation, registration and naming of separate external features of phenomena, empirical knowledge takes the form of specific answers, procedures and solutions. Empirical knowledge asks "what?" and "how?". It is commonly manifested in memorized names, definitions, classifications and lists.

Expansive learning. The learner questions the validity of tasks and problems posed and begins to transform the context itself. This occurs for example when workers analyze critically their work practice and begin to transform it. In such learning processes, internalization steps to the background while externalization of novel practices and ideas gains priority.

External factors of teaching. Directly visible circumstances during the time of teaching, such as the observable behaviour of students, or observable forms of teaching (lecture, group work, etc.). Exclusive attention on external factors makes the immediate reactions of students, such as their approval or disapproval, appear more important than making sense of the contents of instruction.

Instruction. Instruction, or teaching, aims at conscious, goal-directed learning. Its task is to motivate, direct and facilitate studying. Instruction attempts to effectively influence the student's personality. It is typically separated from other activities and protected from disturbing factors. Instruction influences a person's development by means of accumulated and organized knowledge and skills embedded in social practices and artifacts. The main contents of instruction are stored in various forms of representation such as stories, books, pictures, models, instruments and computer programs.

Instructional format. Indicates who is communicating or working at a given moment in instruction. Instructional formats can be divided into three main groups: presentation, independent assignments and cooperative instruction. Instructional formats belong to the external aspect of teaching methods.

Instructional function. The function of the given phase of teaching from the point of view of the students' learning process. The instructor should know which step in the cycle of investigative learning he or she is trying to achieve at any moment in instruction. There are nine instructional functions: preparing; motivating; orientating; conveying and elaborating new knowledge; systematizing; practising; applying; criticizing and evaluating and controlling. Instructional functions are teachers' means for evoking and achieving steps in the cycle of investigative learning. They are the internal aspects of teaching methods.

Instrumental motivation (or alienated motivation). Based either on trying to receive external rewards or on the attempt to avoid failure and punishment. When this is the dominant motive for studying, the student is not primarily interested in the content and usefulness of the subject matter; studying is aimed at "making the grade", getting done with and pulling through.

Internal factors of teaching. Means by which students' mental work and sense-making is guided. Typically neglected or used arbitrarily in the absence of a holistic theory of learning and instruction.

Internalization. The transformation of material, external actions into mental, internal actions. Language and speech play an important role in this process. Language is a tool by which material phenomena and acts are recognized and identified. With the help of language we gradually loosen ourselves from concrete, external means and switch over to performing actions with the help of abstract concepts.

Investigative learning. Learning based on experimentation and problem solving. The learner identifies a problem, reflects upon it and formulates a hypothetical explanation of the principles behind successful solutions. The learner tests the hypothesis and modifies it according to the results, constructing theoretical knowledge of the phenomena under study.

Investigative learning proceeds through successive steps or learning actions which make up a learning cycle. Investigative learning is contextual and collaborative, in other words, it is embedded in a web of meaningful social relations, practical tasks and cultural artifacts.

Learning cycle (also cycle of investigative learning). The cycle of investigative learning consists of six steps or learning actions: (1) motivation, (2) orientation, (3) internalization, (4) externalization, (5) critique and (6) control. The starting point of the learning cycle is a true problem and conflict which occurs in the student's practical activity. A groundwork model of explanation is formed, a hypothesis, an orientation basis, which helps to organize and interpret the whole subject under study. Next the new model must be used in performing concrete tasks, changing surrounding reality and creating new solutions – externalization. The possibility is opened for the student to evaluate critically the model and to control and correct his or her learning. Learning in which some of these steps are weak or absent easily remains superficial and fragmented. Proceeding through the entire cycle provides for flexible and independent performance.

Meaningful learning (also productive learning). Meaningful or productive learning can be observed in situations where a person wants to find out the explanation to a problematic or intriguing phenomenon. The learner is a curious observer and problem-solver. The learner uses tools, books, other people's explanations and other such instruments to explain and resolve the problem. The learner constructs ideas about the world and forms explanatory models of its different phenomena by selecting and interpreting information, by correlating and merging newly acquired material into his or her ongoing activity and earlier construction. Meaningfulness is established when new knowledge, new tasks, run into and merge with the learner's activity and former knowledge.

Methods of instruction (also teaching methods). Methods have an external and an internal aspect. Instructional formats and social modes of instruction belong to the external aspects; instructional functions are the internal aspect.

Models. Relatively stable patterns of thought and action. Models are both mental and material. They are not exclusively individual and private; they are also shared cultural patterns of thought and action.

Modes of discourse. Repertoires of talking, writing and generally communicating meanfully in a community of practice. Each community develops a "social language" of its own over time, with its typical vocabulary and attached typical meanings. Communities of practice also adopt typical "speech genres", routinized expressions and idioms which are repeatedly used.

Orientation basis. The model a person uses to fashion his or her own understanding of something, to evaluate it and to solve tasks connected with it. In instruction, the orientation basis is reconstructed several times. First it is prepared beforehand by the instructor. Next it takes shape in the beginning stages of instruction by means of collaborative analysis and experimentation. Then the orientation basis is gradually internalized. Finally, when applied in practical tasks, it will also be criticized and possibly improved. At first the orientation basis is sketched graphically or represented in external form by other means, including discussion and debate between the students and instructors. It is gradually internalized and represented mentally. There are five types of orientation bases: prototypes, advance organizers, algorithms, systems models and "germ cell" models. A good orientation basis stimulates the independent development and derivation of further complementary orientation bases which illuminate different aspects or parts of a whole.

Productive learning. See meaningful learning.

Situational motivation. The mainly temporary captivation of students' attention by external factors, such as the fascinating novelty of a situation, the characteristics of other participants or the entertaining performance of a teacher.

Social mode of instruction. The manner in which participants are grouped and their interaction is organized in instruction. The following main social modes may be identified: frontal classroom teaching, individual work, work in small groups, work in pairs and sectional work. Social modes belong to the external aspects of teaching methods.

Student tasks. Vehicles for organizing and guiding students' learning activity. For the construction of meaningful tasks, the decisive precondition is the inclusion of context in the tasks. In work-related adult training, tasks should be found in real work settings, genuine communities of practice. Many tasks can actually be performed and solved in such real life settings. Many others must be simulated, reconstructed in classrooms or special workshops. Students should be able to construct the task as part of work activity, not being forced to tackle the task as an isolated exercise.

Substantial motivation. Studying is based on one's interest in the content and usefulness of the subject matter. The student perceives "use value" in mastering and understanding or developing and transforming the practices he or she is engaged in. This is a crucial precondition and component of investigative learning. Substantial motivation arises when the student experiences and recognizes a conflict between his or her knowledge or skill and the requirements of the new task he or she is facing.

Teaching methods. See methods of instruction.

Teaching skill. Internal factors of teaching skill consist of mastery of the instructional contents, mastery of a consistent theory of teaching and learning and mastery of teaching ethics. External factors of teaching skill consist of presentation skills, interpersonal skills, organizational skills and technological skills.

Thematic unit. A relatively independent and complete substantive theme of instruction. The kernel of the thematic unit is some important new theoretical insight or instructionally worthy concept. The contents of the thematic unit are organized in such a way that theoretical insight can be linked to practical application. The duration and scope of the thematic unit must be sufficient to allow for the realization of a complete cycle of investigative learning. Typically a thematic unit covers several successive lessons.

Theoretical knowledge. Based on intervening in phenomena, on setting and testing hypotheses, theoretical knowledge manifests itself in general explanatory models used as means of reaching and formulating variable specific solutions, answers and definitions. The core of theoretical knowledge is to be found in such powerful intellectual procedures as historical analysis, experimentation, detection of contradictions and modelling. Theoretical knowledge asks why the answer was correct, why the solution was successful. In that sense, theoretical knowledge is insatiable. It implies risk taking and uncertainty. It incessantly endeavours to step into unknown territory. Theoretical knowledge has the character of continuous questioning, dialogue and self-revision.

Training. Education aimed at the formation of particular skills and specific competencies is called training.

Zone of proximal development. At the level of an individual learner, the zone of proximal development is the distance between the performance the student is capable of on his or her own and the performance he or she can attain in collaboration with a more knowledgeable or skilled colleague. It is the instructor's responsibility to arrange for the emergence of such zones. At the level of a whole community of practice, the zone of proximal development is a contested area between the traditional practice and alternative future directions.

BIBLIOGRAPHY

Abadzi, H. (1990). *Cognitive Psychology in the Seminar Room*. Washington, D.C.: The International Bank for Reconstruction and Development/The World Bank.

Ames, G. J. & Murray, F. B. (1982). *When two wrongs make a right: Promoting cognitive change by social conflict*. Developmental Psychology 18, 614-623.

Armstrong, R. J. & al. (1970). *The development and evaluation of behavioural objectives*. Worthington: C. A. Jones Publishers.

Ausubel, D. P. (1963). *The psychology of meaningful verbal learning: An introduction to school learning*. New York: Grune & Stratton.

Ausubel, D. P., Novak, J. D. & Hanesian, H. (1978). *Educational psychology: A cognitive view*. New York: Holt, Rinehart & Winston.

Axelrod, R. (Ed.) (1976). *The structure of decision: The cognitive maps of political elites*. Princeton: Princeton University Press.

Bakhtin, M. M. (1981). *The dialogic imagination: Four essays by M. M. Bakhtin*. Austin: University of Texas Press.

Bakhtin, M. M. (1986). *Speech genres and other late essays*. Austin: University of Texas Press.

Bateson, G. (1972). *Steps to an ecology of mind*. New York: Ballantine Books.

Berlyne, D. E. (1960). *Conflict, arousal, and curiosity*. New York: McGraw-Hill.

Becker, H. (1972). *A school is a lousy place to learn anything*. American Behavioural Scientist 16, 85-105.

Billig, M. (1987). *Arguing and thinking: A rhetorical approach to social psychology*. Cambridge: Cambridge University Press.

Billig, M. & al. (1988). *Ideological dilemmas: A social psychology of everyday thinking*. London: Sage.

Boland, Jr., R. J. & al. (1992). *Sharing perspectives in distributed decision making*. In J. Turner & R. Kraut (Eds.), CSCW '92: *Sharing perspectives*. Proceedings of the Conference on Computer-Supported Cooperative Work. October 1992, Toronto, Canada. New York: ACM.

Bransford, J. D. & Johnson, M. K. (1972). *Contextual prerequisites for understanding: Some investigations of comprehension and recall.* Journal of Verbal Learning and Verbal Behaviour 11, 717-720.

Bratus, B. S. (1990). *Anomalies of personality: From the deviant to the norm.* Orlando: Paul M. Deutsch Press.

Brubacher, M., Payne, R. & Rickett, K. (1990). *Perspectives on small group learning: Theory and practice.* Oakville: Rubicon.

Bruner, J. S. (1963). *The process of education.* New York: Vintage Books.

Bruner, J. S. (1966). *Toward a theory of instruction.* Cambridge: Harvard University Press.

Bruner, J. S. (1990). *Acts of meaning.* Cambridge: Harvard University Press.

Butera, F. & Thurman, J. E. (Eds.) (1984). *Automation and Work Design. International Labour Organization.* Amsterdam: Elsevier Science Publishers.

Checkland, P. (1981). *Systems thinking, systems practice.* Chichester: Wiley.

Checkland, P. & Scholes, J. (1990). *Soft systems methodology in action.* Chichester: Wiley.

Clarke, J., Wideman, R. & Eadie, S. (1990). *Together we learn.* Toronto: Prentice-Hall.

Cohen, E. G. (1986). *Designing groupwork: Strategies for the heterogeneous classroom.* New York: Teachers College Press.

Cole, R. E. (1989). *Strategies for learning: Small-group activities in American, Japanese, and Swedish industry.* Berkeley: University of California Press.

Davidson, N. & Worsham, T. (Eds.) (1992). *Enhancing thinking through cooperative learning.* New York: Teachers College Press.

Davydov, V. V. (1988). *Problems of developmental teaching: The experience of theoretical and experimental psychological research.* Parts 1-3. Soviet Education 30(8-10).

Davydov, V. V. (1990). *Types of generalization in instruction.* Reston: National Council of Teachers of Mathematics.

Donald, M. (1991). *Origins of the modern mind: Three stages in the evolution of culture and cognition.* Cambridge: Harvard University Press.

Eisner, E. (Ed.). (1985). *Learning and teaching the ways of knowing.* Eighty-fourth yearbook of the National Society for the Study of Education. Part II. Chicago: NSSE.

Engeström, Y. (1982). *Perustietoa opetuksesta* (Fundamentals of instruction). Helsinki: Valtion painatuskeskus (in Finnish).

Engeström, Y. (1984). *Orientointi opetuksessa* (Orientation in instruction). Helsinki: Valtion koulutuskeskus (in Finnish).

Engeström, Y. (1987). *Learning by expanding: An activity-theoretical approach to developmental research*. Helsinki: Orienta-Konsultit.

Engeström, Y. (1990). *Learning, working and imagining: Twelve studies in activity theory*. Helsinki: Orienta-Konsultit.

Engeström, Y. (1991a). *Developmental work research: Reconstructing expertise through expansive learning*. In M. I. Nurminen & G. R. S. Weir (Eds.), *Human jobs and computer interfaces*. Amsterdam: Elsevier Science Publishers.

Engeström, Y. (1991b). *Non scolae sed vitae discimus: Toward overcoming the encapsulation of school learning*. Learning and Instruction 1, 243-259.

Engeström, Y. (1992). *Interactive expertise: Studies in distributed working intelligence*. University of Helsinki, Department of Education. Research Bulletin 83.

Engeström, Y., Hakkarainen, P. & Hedegaard, M. (1984). *On the methodological basis of research in teaching and learning*. In M. Hedegaard, P. Hakkarainen & Y. Engeström (Eds.), *Learning and teaching on a scientific basis: Methodological and epistemological aspects of the activity theory of learning and teaching*. Aarhus: Aarhus Universitet.

Engeström, Y. & Hedegaard, M. (1985). *Teaching theoretical thinking in primary school: The use of models in history/biology*. In E. Bol, J. P. P. Haenen & M. A. Wolters (Eds.), *Education for cognitive development*. Den Haag: SVO/SOO.

Entwistle, N. (1981). *Styles of learning and teaching*. Chichester: Wiley.

Fichtner, B. (1984). *Co-ordination, co-operation and communication in the formation of theoretical concepts in instruction*. In M. Hedegaard, P. Hakkarainen & Y. Engeström (Eds.), *Learning and teaching on a scientific basis: Methodological and epistemological aspects of the activity theory of learning and teaching*. Aarhus: Aarhus Universitet.

Forrest-Pressley, G. E., MacKinnon, G. E. & Waller, T. G. (Eds.) (1985). *Metacognition, cognition, and human performance*. Orlando: Academic Press.

Freire, P. (1988). *Pedagogy of the oppressed*. New York: Continuum.

Galegher, J., Kraut, R. E. & Egido, C. (Eds.) (1990). *Intellectual teamwork: Social and technological foundations of cooperative work*. Hillsdale: Lawrence Erlbaum.

Gallwey, W. T. (1974). *The inner game of tennis*. New York: Random House.

Gal'perin, P. J. (1969). *Stages in the development of mental acts*. In M. Cole & I. Maltzman (Eds.), A handbook of contemporary Soviet psychology. New York: Basic Books.

Gal'perin, P. J. (1989). *Organization of mental activity and the effectiveness of learning*. Soviet Psychology 27(3), 65-82.

Gal'perin, P. J. (1992). *Stage-by-stage formation as a method of psychological investigation*. Journal of Russian and East European Psychology 30(4), 60-80.

Gardner, H. M. (1983). *Frames of mind: The theory of multiple intelligences*. New York: Basic Books.

Gardner, H. M. (1985). *The mind's new science: A history of the cognitive revolution*. New York: Basic Books.

Gardner, H. M. (1990). *The difficulties of school: Probable causes, possible cures*. Daedalus 119, 85-113.

Garnham, A. (1987). *Mental models as representations of discourse and text*. New York: Halsted Press.

Gentner, D. & Stevens, A. L. (Eds.) (1983). *Mental models*. Hillsdale: Lawrence Erlbaum.

Getzels, J. W. & Csikszentmihalyi, M. (1976). *The creative vision: A longitudinal study of problem finding in art*. New York: Wiley.

Grassel, H. & Bonnke, R. (1977). *Die Lehrertätigkeit als Bedingung für die Lerntätigkeit der Schüler* (Teacher activity as precondition of students' learning activity). In J. Lompscher (Ed.), *Zur Psychologie der Lerntätigkeit*. Berlin: Volk und Wissen (in German).

Greenfield, P. M. (1984). *Mind and media: The effects of television, video games, and computers*. Cambridge: Harvard University Press.

Hakkarainen, P. (1988). *Learning motivation and the theory of activity*. In M. Hildebrand-Nilshon & G. Rückriem (Eds.), Proceedings of the 1st International Congress on Activity Theory. Vol. 3. Berlin: System-Druck.

Hallden, O. (1982). *Elevernas tolkning av skoluppgiften* (Students' interpretation of the school task). Stockholm: Stockholms Universitet, Pedagogiska institutionen (in Swedish).

Harel, I. & Papert, S. (Eds.) (1991). *Constructionism: Research reports and essays, 1985-1990*. Norwood: Ablex.

Harré, R. (1992). *The second cognitive revolution*. American Behavioural Scientist 36, 5-7.

Health & Safety Executive. (1991). *Successful health & safety management*. Health and Safety Series booklet HS(G) 65. London.

Hedegaard, M., Hakkarainen, P. & Engeström, Y. (Eds.) (1984). *Learning and teaching on a scientific basis: Methodological and epistemological aspects of the activity theory of learning and teaching.* Aarhus: Aarhus Universitet.

Hendrick, K. (1990). *Systematic Safety Training.* New York: Marcel Dekker.

Hirschhorn, L. (1984). *Beyond mechanization: Work and technology in a postindustrial age.* Cambridge: The MIT Press.

ILO. (1988). *Major Hazard Control, A practical manual.* Geneva: International Labour Organization.

Jakku-Sihvonen, R. (1981). *Tavoitteisuus ja opettamisprosessi* (Goal-directedness and instructional process). Helsinki: Valtion koulutuskeskus. Tutkimuksia ja selvityksis 1 (in Finnish).

Johnson, D. W. & Johnson, R. (1989). *Cooperation and competition: Theory and research.* Edina: Interaction Book Company.

Jordan, B. & Henderson, A. (1993). *Interaction analysis: Foundations and practice.* Journal of the Learning Sciences (forthcoming).

Judd, C. H. (1908). *The relation of special training to general intelligence.* Educational Review 36, 28-42.

Kagan, S. (1990). *Cooperative learning: Resources for teachers.* San Juan Capistrano: Resources for Teachers.

Kapfer, M. B. (Ed.) (1978). *Behavioural objectives: The position of the pendulum.* Englewood Cliffs: Educational Technology Publications.

Kay, A. C. (1991). *Computers, networks and education.* Scientific American 265(3), 138-148.

Kearsley, G. (1985). *Training for tomorrow: Distributed learning through computer and communications technology.* Reading: Addison Wesley.

Kibler, R. J., Barker, L. L. & Miles, D. T. (1970). *Behavioural objectives and instruction.* Boston: Allyn and Bacon.

Kiviharju, T-J. (1991). *Hoists, lifts and other lifting appliances.* In Timo Leino (Ed.). *Factory Inspection – Selected Technical Papers.* Harare: ILO, African Regional Labour Administration Centre.

Kletz, T. A. (1988). *What Went Wrong? Case Histories of Process Plant Disasters.* Houston: Gulf Publishing Company.

Kolb, D. A. (1984). *Experiential learning: Experience as the source of learning and development.* Englewood Cliffs: Prentice-Hall.

Lakoff, G. & Johnson, M. (1980). *Metaphors we live by.* Chicago: University of Chicago Press.

Landa, L. N. (1974). *Algorithmization in learning and instruction*. Englewood Cliffs: Educational Technology Publications.

Lave, J. & Wenger, E. (1991). *Situated learning: Legitimate peripheral participation*. Cambridge: Cambridge University Press.

Leont'ev, A. N. (1978). *Activity, consciousness, and personality*. Englewood Cliffs: Prentice-Hall.

Lind, G. (1975). *Sachbezogene Motivation im naturwissenschaftlichen Unterricht*. Weinheim: Beltz.

McAshan, H. H. (1970). *Writing behavioural objectives: A new approach*. New York: Harper & Row.

McPeck, J. E. (1990). *Teaching critical thinking: Dialogue and dialectic*. New York: Routledge.

Mager, R. F. (1962). *Preparing instructional objectives*. Palo Alto: Fearon Publishers.

Markova, A. K. (1979). *The teaching and mastery of language*. White Plains: Sharpe.

Markova, I. & Foppa, K. (Eds.) (1990). *The dynamics of dialogue*. New York: Harvester Wheatsheaf.

Marton, F., Hounsell, D. & Entwistle, N. (Eds.) (1984). *The experience of learning*. Edinburgh: Scottish Academic Press.

Mayer, R. E. (1979). *Can advance organizers influence meaningful learning?* Review of Educational Research 49, 371-383.

McNeill, D. (1992). *Hand and mind: What gestures reveal about thought*. Chicago: The University of Chicago Press.

McTighe, J. (1992). *Graphic organizers: Collaborative links to better thinking*. In N. Davidson & T. Worsham (Eds.), *Enhancing thinking through cooperative learning*. New York: Teachers College Press.

Middleton, D. & Edwards, D. (Eds.) (1990). *Collective remembering*. London: Sage.

Miettinen, R. (1993). *Oppitunnista oppimistoimintaan* (From lesson to learning activity). Helsinki: Gaudeamus (in Finnish).

Mills, C. W. (1967). *Power, politics and people: The collected essays of C. Wright Mills*. London: Oxford University Press.

Moll, L. C. (Ed.) (1990). *Vygotsky and education: Instructional implications and applications of sociohistorical psychology*. Cambridge: Cambridge University Press.

Moll, L. C. & Greenberg, J. B. (1990). *Creating zones of possibilities: Combining social contexts for instruction.* In L. C. Moll (Ed.), *Vygotsky and education: Instructional implications and applications of sociohistorical psychology.* Cambridge: Cambridge University Press.

Nelson, T. O. (Ed.) (1992). *Metacognition: Core readings.* Boston: Allyn and Bacon.

Newman, D., Griffin, P. & Cole, M. (1989). *The construction zone: Working for cognitive change in school.* Cambridge: Cambridge University Press.

Norman, D. A. (1980). *Twelve issues for cognitive science.* Cognitive Science 4, 1-32.

Norman, D. A. (1988). *The psychology of everyday things.* New York: Basic Books.

Ortony, A. (Ed.) (1979). *Metaphors and thought.* Cambridge: Cambridge University Press.

Papert, S. (1980). *Mindstorms: Children, computers, and powerful ideas.* New York: Basic Books.

Perret-Clermont, A-N. (1980). *Social interaction and cognitive development in children.* London: Academic Press.

Perret-Clermont, A-N. & Brossard, A. (1985). *On the interdigitation of social and cognitive processes.* In R. A. Hinde, A-N. Perret-Clermont & J. Stevenson-Hinde (Eds.), *Social relationships and cognitive development.* London: Clarendon Press.

Peters, T. (1992). *Liberation management: Necessary disorganization for the nanosecond nineties.* New York: Knopf.

Potter, J. & Wetherell, M. (1987). *Discourse and social psychology: Beyond attitudes and behaviour.* London: Sage.

Powell, W. W. (1990). *Neither market nor hierarchy: Network forms of organization.* In B. M. Staw & L. L. Cummings (Eds.), *Research in organizational behaviour.* Vol. 12. Greenwich: JAI Press.

Raeithel, A. (1983). *Tätigkeit, Arbeit und Praxis.* Frankfurt am Main: Campus.

Reich, R. B. (1992). *The work of nations: Preparing ourselves for 21st century capitalism.* New York: Vintage Books.

Reeve, R. A. & Brown. A. L. (1984). *Metacognition reconsidered: Implications for intervention research.* Cambridge: Bolt, Beranek and Newman.

Resnick, L. B. (1987a). *Education and learning to think.* Washington, DC: National Academy Press.

Resnick, L. B. (1987b). *Learning in school and out.* Educational Researcher 16(9), 13-20.

Resnick, L. B., Levine, J. M. & Teasley, S. D. (Eds.) (1991). *Perspectives on socially shared cognition.* Washington, DC: American Psychological Association.

Riel, M. & Levin, J. (1990). *Building electronic communities: Success and failure in computer networking.* Instructional Science 19, 145- 169.

Roberts, N. & al. (1990). *Integrating telecommunications into education.* Englewood Cliffs: Prentice-Hall.

Rogers, C. R. (1969). *Freedom to learn: A view of what education might be.* Columbus: Merrill.

Rogers, C. R. (1970). *Carl Rogers on encounter groups.* New York: Harper & Row.

Rogers, Y., Rutherford, A. & Bibby, P. A. (Eds.) (1992). *Models in the mind: Theory, perspective and application.* London: Academic Press.

Rorabaugh, W. J. (1986). *The chaft apprentice: From Franklin to the machine age in America.* New York: Oxford University Press.

Rosch, E. & Lloyd, B. B. (Eds.) (1978). *Cognition and categorization.* Hillsdale: Lawrence Erlbaum.

Salomon, G. (1981). *Communication and education: Social and psychological interactions.* Beverly Hills: Sage.

Säljö, R. (1982). *Learning and understanding.* Gothenburg: University of Gothenburg.

Scandura, J. M. (1976). *Structural learning.* New York: Gordon and Breach.

Schön, D. A. (1983). *The reflective practitioner: How professionals think in action.* New York: Basic Books.

Schön, D. A. (1987). *Educating the reflective practitioner: Toward a new design for teaching and learning in the professions.* San Francisco: Jossey-Bass.

Senge, P. M. (1990). *The fifth discipline: The art and practice of the learning organization.* New York: Doubleday.

Sharan, S. (Ed.) (1990). *Cooperative learning: Theory and research.* New York: Praeger.

Sheinker, J. & Sheinker, A. (1989). *Metacognitive approach to study strategies.* Rockville: Aspen Publishers.

Slavin, R. (1990). *Cooperative learning: Theory, research, and practice.* Englewood Cliffs: Prentice-Hall.

Smith, K., Johnson, D. & Johnson, R. (1981). *Can conflict be constructive? Controversy versus concurrence seeking in learning groups.* Journal of Educational Psychology 73, 651-663.

Sutter, B. & Grensjö, B. (1988). *Explorative learning in the school? Experiences of local historical research by the pupils.* The Quarterly Newsletter of the Laboratory of Comparative Human Cognition 10, 39-54.

Talyzina, N. F. (1981). *The psychology of learning.* Moscow: Progress Publishers.

Tharp, R. G. & Gallimore, R. (1988). *Rousing minds to life: Teaching, learning, and schooling in social context.* Cambridge: Cambridge University Press.

Thurman, J. E., Louzine, A. E. & Kogi, K. (1988). *Higher productivity and a better place to work, Action manual.* International Labour Office, Geneva.

Tomasello, M., Kruger, A. C. & Ratner, H. H. (1992). *Cultural learning.* To appear in Behavioural and Brain Sciences.

Vähäpassi, A. (1991). *Hazard Identification and Classification.* In Timo Leino (Ed.). *Factory Inspection – Selected Technical Papers.* Harare: ILO, African Regional Labour Administration Centre (ARLAC).

Vähäpassi, A. (1992). *Changing role of factory inspectors: From enforcement to advisory services.* Course handout. ILO African Safety and Health Project INT/89/M16/FIN.

Vargas, J. S. (1972). *Writing worthwhile behavioural objectives.* New York: Harper & Row.

Virkkunen, J. (1991). *Towards transforming structures of communication in work: The case of Finnish labour protection inspectors.* The Quarterly Newsletter of the Laboratory of Comparative Human Cognition 13, 97-107.

Vygotsky, L. S. (1978). *Mind in society: The development of higher psychological processes.* Cambridge: Harvard University Press.

Weinert, F. E. & Kluwe, R. H. (Eds.) (1987). *Metacognition, motivation, and understanding.* Hillsdale: Lawrence Erlbaum.

Wertsch, J. V. (Ed.) (1981). *The concept of activity in Soviet psychology.* Armonk: M. E. Sharpe.

Wertsch, J. V. (1991). *Voices of the mind.* Cambridge: Harvard University Press.

Whitehead, A. N. (1929). *The aims of education.* New York: MacMillan.

Zankov, L. V. & al. (1977). *Teaching and development: A Soviet investigation.* White Plains: M. E. Sharpe.

Zuboff, S. (1988). *In the age of the smart machine: The future of work and power.* New York: Basic Books.

Picture 1: Advance organizer: The pyramid model of the classification of orientation basis

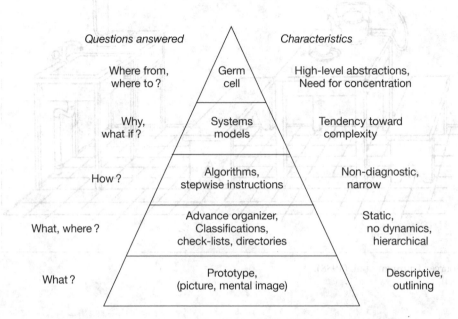

Questions answered		Characteristics
Where from, where to?	Germ cell	High-level abstractions, Need for concentration
Why, what if?	Systems models	Tendency toward complexity
How?	Algorithms, stepwise instructions	Non-diagnostic, narrow
What, where?	Advance organizer, Classifications, check-lists, directories	Static, no dynamics, hierarchical
What?	Prototype, (picture, mental image)	Descriptive, outlining

Source: Engeström (1984).

Picture 2: Prototype: Accident description

1.1.3 Inadequate isolation

A reactor was prepared for maintenance and washed out. There was no welding to be done and no entry was required, so it was decided not to slip-plate off the reactor but to rely on valve isolations. Some flammable vapor leaked through the closed valves into the reactor and was ignited by a high speed abrasive wheel which was being used to cut through one of the pipelines attached to the vessel. The reactor head was blown off and killed two men. It was estimated that 7 kg of hydrocarbon vapor could have caused the explosion.

Following the accident, demonstration cuts were made in the workshop. It was found that as the abrasive wheel broke through the pipe wall, a small flarne occurred and the pipe itself glowed dull red.

The explosion could have been prevented by isolating the reactor by slip-plates or physical disconnection. This incident and the previous one show that valves are not good enough.

Source: Trevor A. Kletz: *What went wrong? Case histories of process plant disasters.* Copyright © 1988 by Gulf Publishing Company, Houston, Texas. Used with permission. All rights reserved.

Picture 3: Prototype: An eating place with simple cooking arrangements

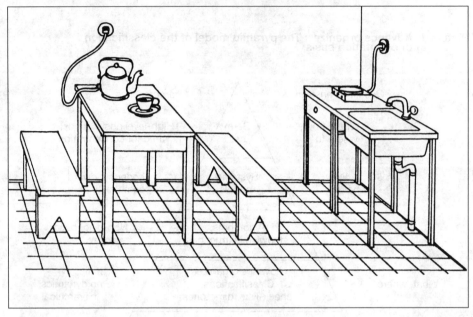

Source: Thurman et al. (1988).

Picture 4: Advance organizer: Telephone directory

Liste alphabétique du personnel arrêtée au 05.03.93
Alphabetical staff list as at 05.03.93

	Téléphone		Bureau
Abakoumoff J. Mme	7826	PUBL	2-10
Abate A.	6322	MULTI	7-52
Abdel Fattah M. Mme	6230	DACTYL	2-71
Abdel-Rahman F.M.	6054	SDG/AFR	R2-81
Abla A. Mme	8578	APPL	6-75
Acero Franco N. Mlle	7422	DACTYL	3-11B
Ackroyd S.E. Mme	6753	AISS	9-3
Adamo K. Mlle	7730	REL OFF	2-155
Addo Yirenki F.	8014/8015	SECURIT	R3-14
Aebischer H. Mme	6551	E/ALP	8-64

Source: ILO (1993).

Picture 5: Advance organizer: Family tree of lifting appliances

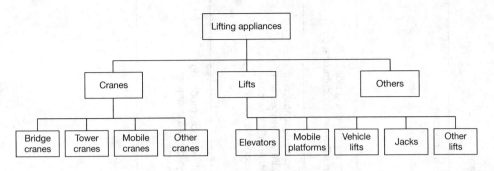

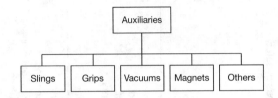

Source: Kiviharju (1991).

Picture 6: Advance organizer: Organization chart

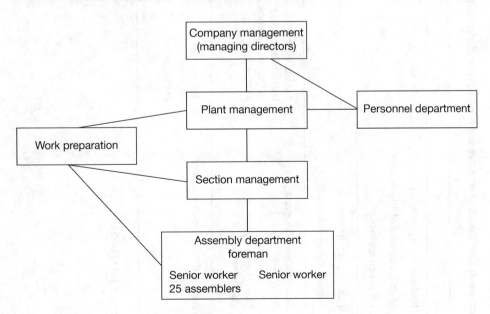

Source: Butera and Thurman (1984).

Picture 7: Combination of advance organizer and algorithm: Working methods for hazard assessment

Method	Purpose	Aim	Working principle
1. Preliminary hazard analysis 2. Matrix diagrams of interactions 3. Use of check-lists	1. Identification of hazards	1. Completeness of safety concept	1. Use of "thinking aids"
4. Failure effect analysis 5. Hazard and operability study			2. Use of "searching aids" and schematic documentation
6. Accident sequence analysis (inductive) 7. Fault tree analysis (deductive)	2. Assessment of hazards according to their occurrence frequency	2. Optimization of reliability and availability of safety systems	3. Graphic description of failure sequences and mathematical calculation of probabilities
8. Accident consequence analysis	3. Assessment of accident consequences	3. Mitigation of consequences and development of optimum emergency plans	4. Mathematical modelling physical and chemical processes

Source: ILO (1988).

Picture 8: Algorithm: Detailed sequence of examination of a vessel

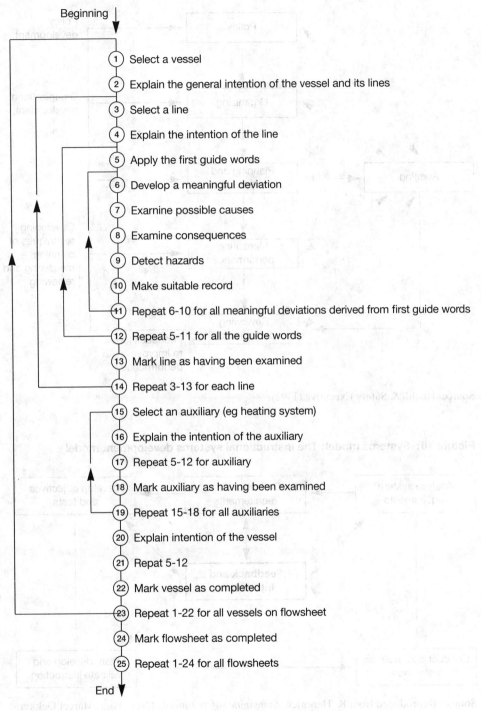

Beginning

1. Select a vessel
2. Explain the general intention of the vessel and its lines
3. Select a line
4. Explain the intention of the line
5. Apply the first guide words
6. Develop a meaningful deviation
7. Examine possible causes
8. Examine consequences
9. Detect hazards
10. Make suitable record
11. Repeat 6-10 for all meaningful deviations derived from first guide words
12. Repeat 5-11 for all the guide words
13. Mark line as having been examined
14. Repeat 3-13 for each line
15. Select an auxiliary (eg heating system)
16. Explain the intention of the auxiliary
17. Repeat 5-12 for auxiliary
18. Mark auxiliary as having been examined
19. Repeat 15-18 for all auxiliaries
20. Explain intention of the vessel
21. Repat 5-12
22. Mark vessel as completed
23. Repeat 1-22 for all vessels on flowsheet
24. Mark flowsheet as completed
25. Repeat 1-24 for all flowsheets

End

Source: ILO (1988).

Picture 9: Systems model: Key elements of successful health and safety management

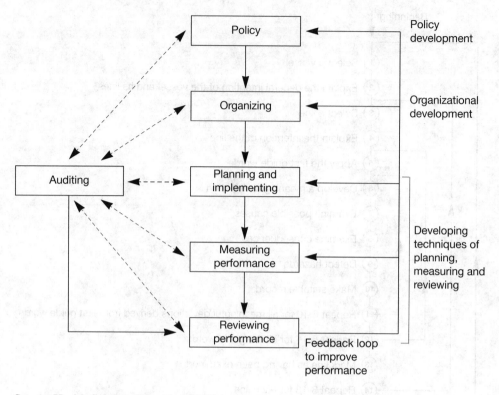

Source: Health & Safety Executive (1992).

Picture 10: Systems model: The instructional systems development model

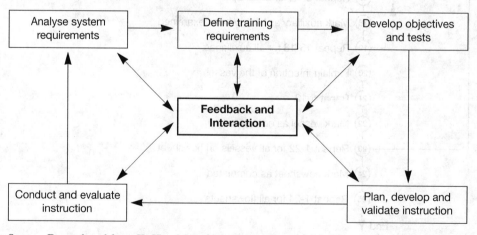

Source: Reproduced from K. Hendrick: *Systematic safety training* (New York, Marcel Dekker, 1990), p. 11, by courtesy of Marcel Dekker Inc.

Picture 11: Systems model: A general systems model

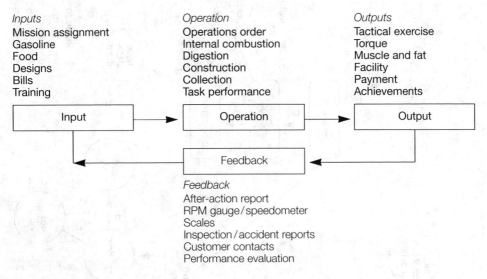

Inputs
Mission assignment
Gasoline
Food
Designs
Bills
Training

Operation
Operations order
Internal combustion
Digestion
Construction
Collection
Task performance

Outputs
Tactical exercise
Torque
Muscle and fat
Facility
Payment
Achievements

Input → Operation → Output

Feedback

Feedback
After-action report
RPM gauge / speedometer
Scales
Inspection / accident reports
Customer contacts
Performance evaluation

Source: Hendrick, op. cit.

Picture 12: Systems model: Nutritious functions

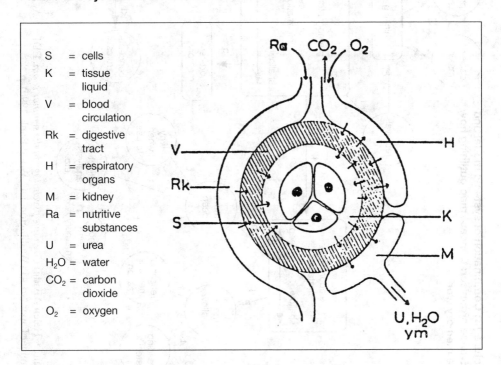

S   = cells
K   = tissue liquid
V   = blood circulation
Rk = digestive tract
H   = respiratory organs
M   = kidney
Ra = nutritive substances
U   = urea
H_2O = water
CO_2 = carbon dioxide
O_2 = oxygen

Source: Engeström (1984).

Picture 13: Combination of systems model and advance organizer: Concept map outlining how the memory works

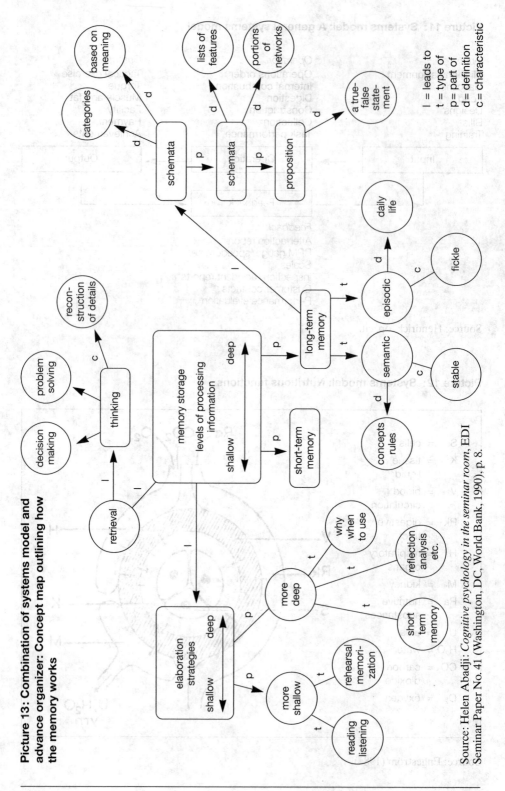

l = leads to
t = type of
p = part of
d = definition
c = characteristic

Source: Helen Abadji: *Cognitive psychology in the seminar room*, EDI Seminar Paper No. 41 (Washington, DC, World Bank, 1990), p. 8.

Picture 14: The investigative learning cycle

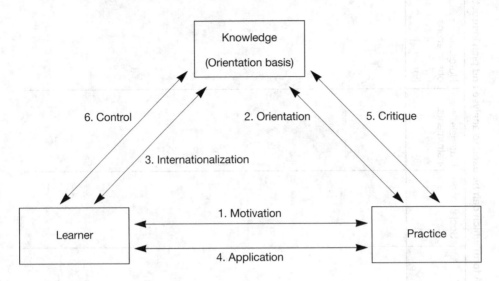

Source: Engeström, Hakkarainen and Hedegaard (1984).

Picture 15: Germ cell: Accident model (c)

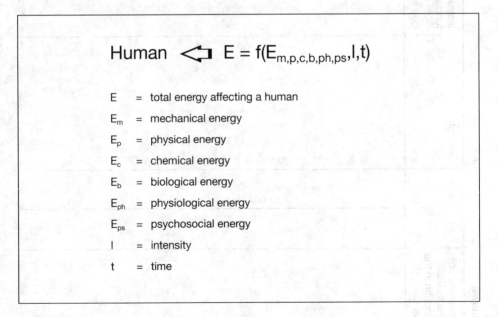

$$\text{Human} \Leftarrow E = f(E_{m,p,c,b,ph,ps}, I, t)$$

E	=	total energy affecting a human
E_m	=	mechanical energy
E_p	=	physical energy
E_c	=	chemical energy
E_b	=	biological energy
E_{ph}	=	physiological energy
E_{ps}	=	psychosocial energy
I	=	intensity
t	=	time

Source: Vähäpassi (unpublished).

Picture 16: A form which can be used to analyse and plan instruction

Course:

Thematic unit and its main function in the course (1)	Period (2)	Time (3)	Contents (4)	Instructional function (5)	Instructional format (6)	Social mode (7)	Materials, instruments (8)	Notes, observations (9)